MW00993060

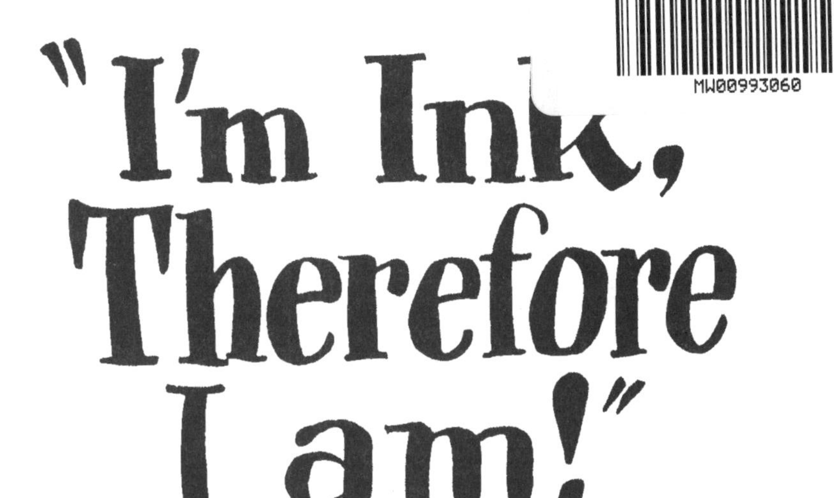

Farley's San Francisco Chronicles

By Phil Frank

Pomegranate
SAN FRANCISCO

This book is dedicated to Stan Arnold—former manager of Chronicle Features and Sunday editor of the *San Francisco Chronicle*—whose insight and sense of humor aided many a cartoonist, including myself. Thanks, Stan.

Published by Pomegranate
Box 6099, Rohnert Park, CA 94927

Pomegranate Europe Ltd.
Fullbridge House, Fullbridge
Maldon, Essex CM9 7LE, England

© 1997 Phil Frank

All rights reserved.

No part of this book may be reproduced or transmitted in any form or by any means, electronic or mechanical, including photocopying, recording, or by any information storage and retrieval system, without permission in writing from the copyright holders.

ISBN 0-7649-0358-6
Pomegranate Catalog No. A889

All artwork by Phil Frank

Library of Congress Catalog Card Number 97-67617

Printed in Canada
06 05 04 03 02 01 00 99 98 97 10 9 8 7 6 5 4 3 2 1

First Edition

OFFICE OF THE MAYOR
SAN FRANCISCO

WILLIE LEWIS BROWN, JR.

No one has given me more hell, or more laughs, in recent years than Phil Frank. I've always enjoyed Phil's wonderful cartoon strip, but ever since I became the Mayor of San Francisco, that little ink well sitting on his desk has forced me to keep a clean conscience as well as a keen sense of humor. The people of San Francisco – particularly my clergyman – owe "Farley" a debt of gratitude.

Like my good friend, the late great Herb Caen, whose *Chronicle* column focused on daily life in San Francisco for so many years, Phil Frank is a cartoon chronicler of such exquisite taste that for more than a decade now he's concentrated solely on the wild and wacky world of Baghdad by the Bay ... and the City has been all the richer for his wit and incisive humor.

We are truly lucky to have a daily comic strip that caters entirely to us, the people of the San Francisco Bay Area. And we're especially lucky to have Phil Frank as its creator – he keeps "Farley" timely, insightful, biting and, above all, funny. When it comes to "Farley," even a moving target like me has to tip his hat.

Mayor Willie L. Brown, Jr.

401 VAN NESS AVENUE, ROOM 336, SAN FRANCISCO, CALIFORNIA 94102
(415) 554-6141
RECYCLED PAPER

The Setting: The hilly city of San Francisco teetering on the edge of the Pacific Plate, existing both in reality and imagination. It's populated in real life by individuals doing the most peculiar things, providing me with material enough to last a millennium.

The other San Francisco that exists solely on my drawing board is inhabited by highly evolved urbanized black bears, sensuous meter maids, fast-talking feral felines, a right-winged raven, a trio of porcine bad boys in a BMW, a cyberswami named Baba, an undercover cop named Tuslo, a homeless entrepreneur and a procession of mayors to rule the lot.

The common thread that ties this motley crew together is the fearless (though sometimes fearful) Farley, intrepid reporter for San Francisco's morning paper.

My goal through 22 years of putting Farley in print was to soften this world's sometimes harsh headlines using humor as an antidote.

A beacon cuts through the night sky, shining a big drip on the city's fog bank. It is a signal that calls to action that famous water saver, Frugal Faucet – who, disguised as a mild-mannered reporter for a metropolitan paper, fights a never-ending battle against leaks, drips and American waste.

FASTER THAN A SPEEDING PULLET! MORE POWERFUL THAN A LOCO MOTIVE..
I'm helping..
SQUAAAWK!
2-9-91

..ABLE TO LEAP TALL BUILDING MANAGERS IN A SINGLE BOUND..
YOUR RENT'S LATE, FARLEY!

HE FIGHTS A NEVER-ENDING BATTLE AGAINST WATER WASTE!
ZOUNDS! A GUTTER FLOODER!
GRRR!
Look out, Frugal!! He's got a hose!
© Phil (THIS IS YOUR VINYL WARNING)

Touch that spigot and you're wet meal, Frugal!
Ha!! Your weapons are useless against me. My cape is waterproof!

OVER IN MARIN COUNTY THE DROUGHT NEWS IS BLEAK. WATER USE MUST BE CUT BY 50%. STIFF PENALTIES WILL GO INTO EFFECT MARCH 1.
USE A HOSE. GO TO JAIL.
MARIN MUNICIPAL WATER DISTRICT

ALLOTMENTS MUST BE CUT BY 50% OF 1986 USEAGE.
Uh.. we didn't live here in 1986 so we don't have a 1986 level.
So you don't get any water.
2-11-91

WATER CONSERVATION TIPS WILL HAVE TO BE RELEARNED.
The bricks go in the tank not the bowl!
© Phil (WATER ON MY BRAIN) Frank

COMMERCIAL LANDSCAPERS WILL BE HIT HARDEST WITH AN 85% REDUCTION!
Easy! Easy! Don't gulp it!

THE FIRST WEEK OF WATER RATIONING IS UNDER WAY IN THE BAY AREA AND CITIZENS BEGIN TO ADAPT... ..AT HOME..
Call me when the rinse cycle is over.

..IN RESTAURANTS..
Waiter! Another water, please!!
3-5-91

..AT WORK..
HEY! WHOSE SOCKS ARE THESE?
© Phil (IS THIS DRIP DRY?) Frank

..AND IN BARS:
I've got an extra water allotment. Want to do a load of wash?

Art Agnos is mayor in 1991, as he was when the earthquake hit in 1989. The earthquake was the zenith of Art's political star. Now, in the spring of 1991 his support, and that of the quake-damaged Embarcadero Freeway, is crumbling.

More, Nostrildamus!! Tell me more about the fall election!
I see... four challengers strong.
Behind them comes a throng..
2-28-91

A supervisor, a latin nightclub owner and a crow will run.
Ethnics four, lesbians two, a man on skates dressed as a nun.

A reporter with an eyepatch will join in from New York..
A punk with green hair, a Communist, and Judge Bork.
©Phil (WEED IT AND REAP) Frank
A Kennedy will run and a man with a bad toupee...
..A gypsy accordionist and a woman named Lupe...
So, it'll be a normal election..

IT IS WEDNESDAY MORNING AND A SPIRITED CROWD GATHERS AT THE HOWARD STREET BASE OF THE EMBARCADERO FREEWAY..
2-27-91

THE MAYOR MARKS THE START OF THE DEMOLITION BY BREAKING A BOTTLE OF CHAMPAGNE AGAINST THE BASE OF A PILLAR..

CREEEEEEAK..
GROOOOOAN
Oh oh..
© Phil (LITE WINE FEVER) Frank
CREEEE
Next time we use a light wine.
Yes, sir.

CHUNK-A! CHUNK-A! CHUNK-A! CHUNK-A!
This is really unusual, isn't it, Mom?
They're usually going up, not down, Olive.

Did you read that the Arts Commision is considering a proposal to leave standing two small sections of the approach ramps as a monument?
4-26-91
CHUNK-A! CHUNK-A!
Well... aren't we well read?

Can't you just see people marveling at it in a thousand years and wondering what it was used for?
CHUNK-A! CHUNK-A!
Hmm..
©Phil (THEY WORSHIPPED THEIR GODS HERE?) Frank

CEMENTHENGE

It's spring and Farley's alter ego, his bird Bruce D. Raven, has taken wing from the SoMa loft that he shares with Farley. He seeks out his true love, Lenore.

In an aerial ballet over Golden Gate Park, the two birds meet and mate, and soon afterward the inevitable takes place.

BIRD-WATCHING ACTIVITY IS AT A PEAK AS ORNITHOLOGISTS GATHER IN SAN FRANCISCO TO STUDY A RARE SIGHT..
Oooo
Ahhh..
Oooo

A PAIR OF CLIFF-DWELLING RAVENS ARE BUILDING A TREE NEST IN THE SUNSET DISTRICT.
3-8-91

WHAT THE BIRD-WATCHERS DO NOT REALIZE IS THAT THE PAIR IS UNDER THE WATCHFUL GAZE OF A CITY BUILDING INSPECTOR, A RED-VESTED NITPICKER.
© Phil (NO GROUT ABOUT IT.) Frank

Here comes the male. He's carrying some nest building materials.. What is it?
Uh... Sheetrock, I believe.

You certainly have gotten testy of late, love..
Testy? TESTY? Do you KNOW what we're paying for this little love nest?
3-15-91

On top of that I've got a Red-Vested Nitpicker for a building inspector who's making me build with sheetrock!
Tsk.. Tsk..

I'm doing this nesting thing just to show Farley that a relationship doesn't have to be complicated or scary..
What? I thought it was because you loved me.
© Phil (MISSOURI LOVES COMPANY) Frank

LATER FOR YOU, BRUCE!
BABYCAKES!!
I WANT GALVANIZED NAILS IN THOSE 2X4's!!
Hee.. Hee..

What's that sound, Farley?
That, Irene, is the sound of a bird pecking on the window.
PECK! PECK! PECK!

If you're looking for Bruce, he doesn't live here anymore. He's built a nest in the Sunset district ..out near Judah and 33rd..
I'M BRUCE!
3-21-91

Where's the love of your life, big bird? I thought you'd be nesting by now.. ..showing me how easy a commitment can be.
There were a few problems.. We had a spat. Let me in!
© Phil (LOVE ME OR LEASE ME.) Frank
Can't. I rented your cage.
Dang! Who do I know on the Rent Board?

Spring is in the air and the bears will soon be coming out of hibernation. The rains have diminished, the hills are green, and deep beneath the **Fog City Dumpster** ("Where the Elite With Four Feet Meet to Eat") our furry friends are waking from their long winter slumber.

THE RECENTLY AWAKENED BEARS TRY TO GET BACK UP TO SPEED AFTER A FOUR-MONTH HIBERNATION:
Hey! The N.Y. Giants beat the Bills 20-19 in the Super Bowl!
There was a big freeze at Christmas!

The Embarcadero Freeway's being torn down!!
THATCHER RESIGNED!
Ronnie Lott Leaves 49ers!!
YOW! MASSIVE SCHOOL CUTBACKS!
4-6-91

WAS THERE A WAR IN THE GULF?
Uh.. YES!! 100 hours long.
Supervisors declare San Francisco a sanctuary.
It's been raining for weeks!
© Phil (WORDS FLAIL ME) Frank

29¢ stamps!!
Michael Jackson Bought by Sony!
Whoa! Media overload.
Domestic Partners Passes!
$450,000 PAID FOR HONUS WAGNER BASEBALL CARD!

FED, RESTED AND RELAXED, THE BEARS EMERGE FROM HIBERNATION INTO THE BRIGHT SPRING SUNSHINE:
FOG CITY DUMPSTER
LOOK!
GIRTH FIRST!
4-8-91

THEY STARE IN DISBELIEF DOWN HOWARD STREET AT THE BAY.
The Embarcadero Freeway...
It's gone.

And the city's been declared a nature sanctuary!
We're protected! We can do or have anything we want!!
I want a bagel!
© Phil (QUICHE AND TELL) Frank

Yo! It's not a nature sanctuary. It's a sanctuary for people opposed to war.
Oh. Bummer!
Hmm.
Keep the bagel!
RTH

TODAY IS OPENING DAY OF THE REGULAR SEASON FOR BOTH THE GIANTS AND THE A's. ALPHONSE ARRIVES AT SECTION 5 AT CANDLESTICK:
YO!!
YO, ALPHONSE!!

Where you been, dude?
Hibernating! Nothing like a four-month nap to get you ready for baseball. Where've you all been since the end of last season?
GIANTS!

Uh.. right here.
4-9-91
© Phil (GIANTS FEVER BLISTERS) Frank

Yeah. We wanted to get good seats. Less than a week now 'til the first home game!
Serious fans..

A MODERN-DAY FAIRY TALE:
IN SPITE OF WHAT APPEARED TO BE 'IRRECONCILABLE DIFFERENCES' OUR RAVEN DUET IS REUNITED:
PET THERAPY
Hey! What about your bill?

THEY IMMEDIATELY PROCEED WITH THE RAVEN RITE OF SPRING... THE REDECLARING OF THEIR VOWS IN THEIR AERIAL MATING DANCE:
4-25-91

THE BUILDING INSPECTOR, A "RED-VESTED NIT PICKER", HAS BEEN BOUGHT OFF WITH A 2 POUND SACK OF MEALWORMS. THEIR SUNSET DISTRICT ABODE IS APPROVED FOR OCCUPANCY.
© Phil (EGG ROLLS?) Frank

WITHIN DAYS "BABYCAKES" IS, AS ORNITHOLOGISTS ARE WONT TO SAY, "WITH BIRD". SHE KNITS CROW BOOTIES AS HER MATE BRINGS HER PILFERED TIDBITS.
Chinese okay?

THE NOISE LEVEL HAS INCREASED NOTICEABLY IN THE NEIGHBORHOOD OF THE RAVENS' NEST:
That's five! They're all hatched.
And hungry.
CHEEEP!

Healthy lungs..
Good voices..
CHEEEP! CHEEEP! CHEEEP!
5-16-91

ADULT RAVENS ARE RECOGNIZED FOR THEIR STATURE AND PLUMAGE. YOUNG RAVENS ARE NOT THUS BLESSED.
BOY! They sure are uggggly!
CHEEEEP! CHEEEEP! CHEEP!
© Phil (PRE MOLTING SYNDROME?) Frank

I noticed it immediately, too.. ..their resemblance to your side of the family.
Post-partum depression, no doubt. Better let that one slide..
CHEEEP! CHEEEP!

SURVIVAL IN THE CITY... ..FIVE YOUNG RAVENS AWAIT THEIR BREAKFAST:
Maybe daddy will find you a nice gopher..
CHEEEP! CHEEEP! CHEEEP!

One order of sourdough pancakes for the Doberman in the corner booth.
5-17-91

You got it!

?
© Phil (ELIOT NEST) Frank

Sourdough pancakes!! How'd you..
Dnt esk..
CHEEP! CHEEP!

Could I have your attention, please? Your mother and I are quite pleased at how well you've turned out..
6-7-91

It's been a month now since you hatched, and your gestation period is almost complete..
? ? ? ? ?

In other words... the free lunch is over. From now on you're on your own.
(© Phil Frank (DOTS ALL, FOLKS!)

Does this by any chance mean the free breakfast and dinner are over too?
As you leave,, take a map of San Francisco. The red dots mark good scavenging spots..

Out at the ravens' nest one of the fledglings has returned:
I don't like it out there!! It's a bird-eat-bird world!!
6-20-91

I don't feel like I've been properly prepared for the grim realities of modern day life in an urban environment!

Somebody didn't do their job!!
What about your four brothers and sisters, Herbie? They're off on their own!!
© Phil Frank (Put in your pecking order)

Oh, right. Drag them out as examples of how I should be. You always liked them better!!

Out at the ravens' nest in the Sunset District, the returned fledgling is starting to rule the roost.
I'm not going! I haven't been properly prepared for urban survival!
6-21-91

We've hatched you, fed you, given you everything you needed including flight lessons and the skills to survive.

Hmmph!

Your mother and I have worked very hard to make you what you are today, young fellow!

Yeah!.. an emotional wreck!
© Phil Frank (And it ain't cheep!)

Maybe it's a ploy to get us to pay his way through grad school...

It's a one-sided love affair that goes back some twenty years. He was a seasonal ranger at Asphalt State Park. She was the matriarch of the bear clan. She had a thing about men in uniforms. The ranger and the bear met. She fell in love. She studied the women he was attracted to. Then she shaves her legs.

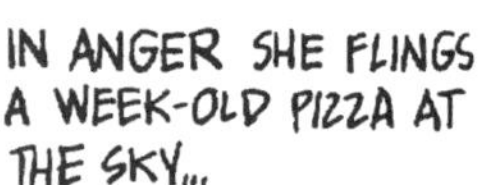

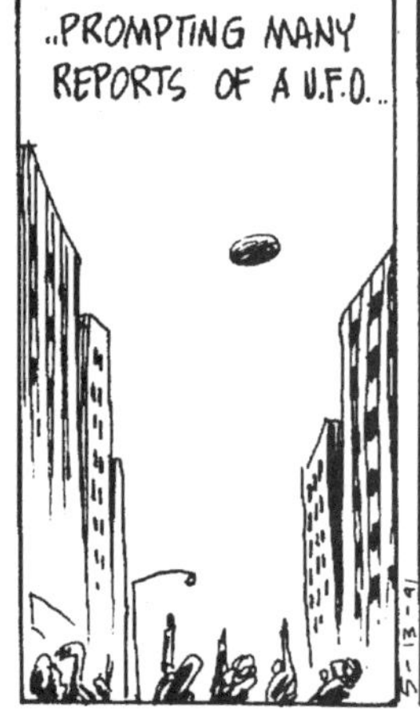

A PSYCHIC CONSULTANT WHO IS JUST OPENING HIS SHOP WITNESSES THE U.F.O.'S LANDING:

WHAP!

I'm not sure what it was I just saw, but whatever it was I'm sure that he deserved it.

FAX BABA

The streets of San Francisco can be tough on humans and animals alike.

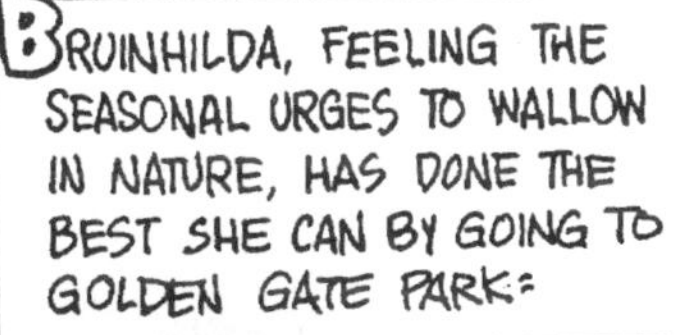

IT'S LATE AT NIGHT AT THE THIRD & TOWNSEND RV PARK IN THE HEART OF THE CITY:
Well, Leo... it's not too woodsy, but it sure is handy for seeing San Francisco..
W

7-17-91
To tell you the truth, Myrna... I'm glad to have a break from the woodsy wildlife..
Care for some Macadamia nuts?

Those pesky raccoons, skunks, possums...
We'll have to go to the zoo to see wildlife now..
©Phil TRICK OR TROUT!:) Frank
Who could be knocking on our door at this hour?
I'll get it.
Remember what to say?
Give us the Macadamia nuts and nobody gets hurt..

Farley.. you want to cover this story?
I'm a columnist now. I don't cover stories. What's it about?

Well... two bears were sighted at an RV park last night..
That's not news!
..At Third and Townsend Street.
That's news!

The police are searching for them now.. Thought you might like to know.. Just in case there's any one who might be interested in that news...
Uh.. yeah. Thanks for the tip..
7-18-91
©Phil THIS BUG'S FOR YOU! Frank

OPEN UP!! I KNOW YOU'RE IN THERE!
BANG!
BANG!
DUMPSTER
Nobody here but us earwigs..
CLOSED

Look! We didn't threaten anyone.. We were just nosing around the RV park south of Market Street.
According to the police report..

"At 10:25 p.m. on the night of Wednesday, July 17th, two California Black Bears pounded on the door of a 1986 Winnebago owned by a Mr. and Mrs. Leo Rootlieb of Chico...
So? Is that a crime?

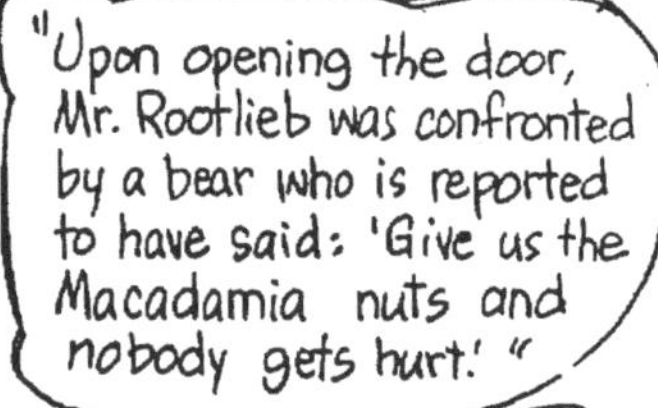
"Upon opening the door, Mr. Rootlieb was confronted by a bear who is reported to have said: 'Give us the Macadamia nuts and nobody gets hurt.'"

Ahem!
Er...
FOG CITY
DUMPSTER
7-19-91
©Phil (WRITE IF YOU GET WORMS.:) Frank

EYHOUND
Two one-way tickets to Yosemite, please.

When our urbanized black bears (URSUS CORRUPTUS) close up their eatery, the Fog City Dumpster, and head for the woods they take along a lot of baggage. Because I do a lot of artwork for Yosemite National Park, I get a lot of input from rangers and staff. I used some of that input for this series.

SPEAKING THE LANGUAGE OF SIGN AND SYMBOL, OLAF, THE OLD BEAR OF YOSEMITE, COMMUNICATES WITH HIS URBAN COUSINS:
What's he saying, Hilda?
"Many years ago..
7-27-91

"The valley was untouched by human hands...Our forebears lived happily...
"These times are behind us.

Then the horse with wheels brings many paleface visitors who park on nature..
This began in the year 35 B.C.
© Phil (MEGABITE) Frank

B.C.?
Before Cheetos.

HILDA AND ALPHONSE STUDY THE FLORA AND FAUNA OF YOSEMITE:
Any birds, Hilda?
The valley's crawling with wildlife, Alphonse.
7-29-91

I can just see inside the bar at Yosemite Village..
Oooo!! Oooo!!
What is it?

A Great-Horned Bachelor. He's doing a mating dance around a European Starling!
Really?
©Phil (NATURE IS A MOTHER!) Frank

Ooo!! Ooo!! A Buffle-Headed Bully!! ..the Starling's boyfriend just showed up!
who says nature isn't any fun?

ALPHONSE GETS A YOSEMITE NATURE LESSON:
Look, Alphonse!! A Big-Bellied Sudsucker!!
I see it!! Under the pine tree!
7-30-91

Here's what the book says: "This chunky, large-bellied bird is found in park areas near any source of distilled spirits...
ZZZZ
He's not moving...

"It has a ruffled look. Its plumage usually incorporates a rock band t-shirt. Its nest is littered with shiny objects (beer cans) to attract females of the species. Its call is a hoarse "ROCK N' ROLL!" followed by a zigzag flight. Then it lands...

"They are common to campgrounds during the summer season, are given a wide berth by other species and return home when their money runs out."
Still not moving..
©Phil (The Bud Stops Here.) Frank

INSIDE THE GROCERY STORE AT YOSEMITE VILLAGE:
Say.. don't you own that Winnebago with the satellite dish?
Yes! You must own that Trailbuster with the retractable roof. I'm Helen.

8-2-91
I'm Marilyn. Say, did you hear the news that bears have been sighted in the valley?
I saw it on TV. We're trying to figure out how to put our refrigerator up in a tree.

You'd think they'd be afraid of civilization.
The newscaster said they go straight for where the food is.
© Phil (A STICKY SITUATION) Frank
AISLE THREE! PRICE CHECK ON THE 20 GALLON CAN OF HONEY!
Oh, oh..

THERE'S BIG EXCITEMENT AT THE YOSEMITE GOLF COURSE:
BEARS!!
HELP!!
3
8-3-91

Oh, boy!! I've always wanted to try golf..

This is fun!!
WHACK!
Hey, Hilda, Company.

SHOO!! YOU CAN'T COME HERE AND..
GRRRRR!!
Oh, oh.. somebody forgot the first rule of the woods.. "Never get between a bear and her clubs."

Don't take this the wrong way, Hilda.. ..I'm having a great time here..
Hmm?
8-5-91

I just have this odd feeling that the Giants need me right now.. ..pulling for them when they're down..

Stuck in last place, their pitching a shambles, their hitting a disgrace.. their fielding..
I found last Friday's Chronicle in a dumpster yesterday.
© Phil (AND THE BEAST GOES ON) Frank

They'd won 11 games straight and were in fourth place.
Oh, sure. And Kim Basinger was named manager, right?

The Giants in Fourth place? Ha! Ha! You lie like a bear rug, Hilda.
Go find a newspaper if you don't believe me, knucklehead!
9-6-91

Don't think I'm going down to Yosemite Village to get a newspaper so **you** can have a big furry laugh, little miss practical joker!!
I'm going because I want a banana fudge sundae!!

An 11 game winning streak, eh? Ha!! I say! You have to get up pretty darn early to fool **this** bear, you Furry Freak Sister!!
© Phil (SOUNDS MORE LIKE BIT-O-HONEY.) Frank
Those better not be stifled snickers I hear coming from yon Ponderosa pines!!

THE NEWS THAT BEARS HAVE BEEN SIGHTED IN YOSEMITE FINDS CAMPERS TAKING EXTRA PRECAUTIONS:
HANG YOUR FOOD PACKS IN THE TREES.. I REPEAT...
8-23-91

THE PARK SERVICE IS NOW RECOMMENDING THAT CAMPERS TAKE A "MILDLY AGGRESSIVE" TACK WHEN BEARS ENTER THEIR CAMPSITES:
Don't run. Stand your ground. Bang pots, ring bells and yell.

Hey, Alphonse! Been to the campground?
Yeah. What a bummer. All the food's in the trees.
© Phil (THEY'RE BANGING OUR SONG) Frank
Not only that but a steel drum band is camping there and.. Boy!.. ..are they lousy!!
?

Hilda!! Where are you? We need you here! This place is a zoo!!

Alphonse and I are at Tuolumne Meadows. We're calling you on a car phone.
9-12-91

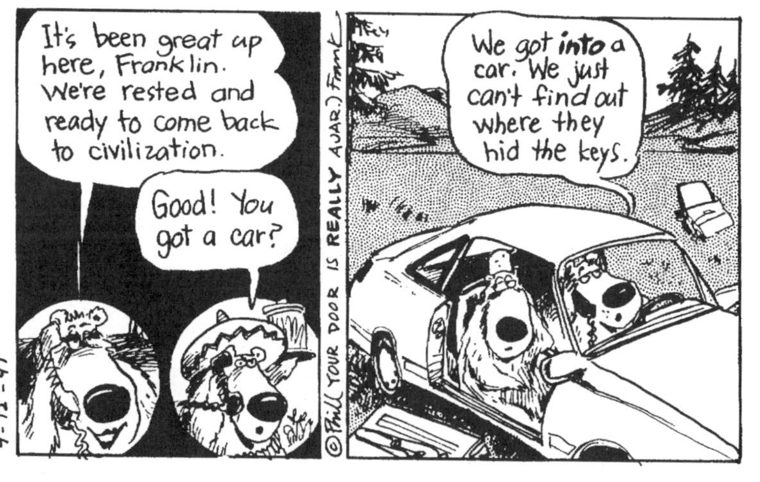
It's been great up here, Franklin. We're rested and ready to come back to civilization.
Good! You got a car?
© Phil (YOUR DOOR IS REALLY AJAR.) Frank
We got **into** a car. We just can't find out where they hid the keys.

Irene the meter maid... honed and a little hardened by her life on the streets of San Francisco. There is a mysterious magnetism between Farley and his career ticket-giver. As penance for his inability to commit to the relationship, she makes him pay by constantly ticketing his Chrysler Rebate.

You wanted me to compromise my job as a Parking Control Officer..
No... baby... Noooo
BEEP!!
HONK!!

You wanted me to rig the San Francisco Fair's "Impossible Parking Space Race" so you could win and get a good column out of it!
It would only be a joke!!
7-25-91

Soliciting an officer and rigging a public contest is not a joke. It's a crime..
I'd refuse the prize, Irene!! It was just a great idea...
© Phil (LIFE IN THE FAST LANE) Frank
You have the right to remain silent... Anything you say..
Maybe it wasn't such a great idea..

Where's Farley, Olive?
He had to go to the bathroom.
9-18-91

I think he feels kind of uncomfortable – this being an all-female household. We were talking about the differences between men and women.
Really?

Did you talk about the little things that most aggravate women about men?
Yes... but we'll have to see if he gets the hint.

PUT THE LID DOWN !!!
© Phil (I NEVER PROMISED YOU A ROSE BOWL.) Frank
CLUNK!
He got it.

Maybe relationships between meter maids and journalists aren't meant to work out..
What are you basing that on?

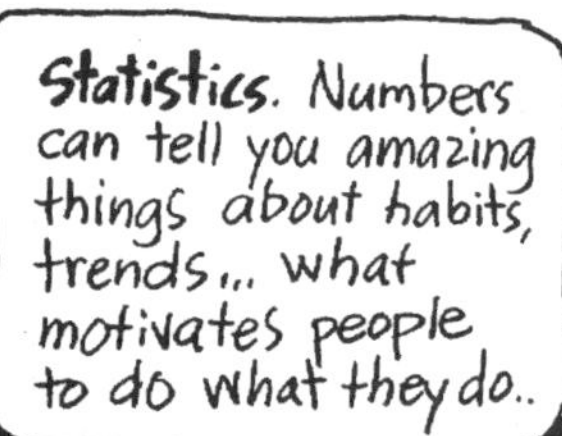
Statistics. Numbers can tell you amazing things about habits, trends... what motivates people to do what they do..

Let's hear it.
9-20-91

Let's see... well out of 87 million two-income relationships in the U.S. the number of journalists married, living with or emotionally involved with meter maids.. hmm..
hmm what?
© Phil (E PLURIBUS DUO) Frank

Nationally speaking... ...we're it.
Great!

Tell me something, Farley.. What's **really** important in your life?
What's **really** important in my life? Umm... baseball.
9-23-91

Baseball??
Yeah, baseball. Double-header against the Dodgers at the 'Stick. Couple of Polish dogs, a beer, peanuts. Humm, baby.
© Phil (OUT AT FIRST) Frank

You were **supposed** to say **I'm** what's really important in your life!!
Oh. Was it a trick question?

I'm seeing you in a new light, Farley. I didn't realize that our relationship was so low on your list of priorities..
9-26-91

I thought you were a caring, sensitive individual.
I **am** caring and sensitive, Irene... ..to a point.
© Phil (WITH THIS CUE, I THEE BLED.) Frank

Face the fact, ma'am, that he's a guy... he cares, ..but more about sports than relationships..
And he's sensitive too, miss. Hit him with my pool cue. See if he doesn't cry out. See if he doesn't bleed.
Uh... gentlemen..

Look, Irene... while we're prattling on about our relationship life is going on out there in the world!
I know that!
9-30-91

Governments are toppling! Scientific breakthroughs are happening! Eight people were just sealed inside the Biosphere in Arizona!!
Locked inside a sealed living unit for two years..

No way to avoid each other or their interpersonal relationships..
Hmm..
I always worry when she says "Hmmm."
© Phil (MISSOURI LOVES COMPANY.) Frank

Farley... have you ever been to Arizona?
See?

You're avoiding the issue of our relationship!
I am **not**! I just feel I've said all I can say on the subject!

10-1-91
I love you but I don't want to get married. If you want me you'll have to take me as I am.

Well.. **I** don't want to be your eternal girlfriend!!
Then it looks like we have a stalemate.
©Phil (WHO YOU CALLIN' A STALE MATE?) Frank
You should consider how this will all affect me later in life, Farley.
Great. Tag-team therapy..

I'm going now.
So.. **GO!** See if I care! Go back to your divine bachelor's pad!

SLAM!
P.N.S.
What?
10-3-91

Pre-Nuptial Syndrome. ..Irritability... ..short temper.. ..crabbiness..
©Phil (A CHILD THERAPIST) Frank

I AM **NOT** CRABBY!!
Need I say more?

BRUCE ARRIVES FROM ARIZONA JUST AS FARLEY WRAPS UP HIS BACHELOR RANT:
Boy! Are my wings tired.
I **LIKE** BEING A BACHELOR!

10-4-91
WOMEN ALWAYS WANT TO CHANGE MEN. I DON'T **WANT** TO CHANGE!

I **like** keeping old pizza in my fridge! Dirty dishes do **not** bother me! The only good plant is a **dead** plant!!
©Phil (SEATS ME FINE) Frank

FROM NOW ON THE TOILET SEAT STAYS **UP**!!
SLAM!
Welcome home.

EVEN IN THE TRENDIEST OF EATERIES THERE IS OCCASIONALLY AN UNSATISFIED CUSTOMER:
WAITER!!
10-10-91

Is there a problem, sir?
YES!! I ordered liverwurst. What is **this**?

I believe that is a piece of liver, sir...
Well?
© PHIL (O PUN THE WINDOW!) FRANK

Apparently.. ..the wurst is yet to come.
?

INSIDE THE CUBICLE OF ***THE DAILY REQUIREMENT***'S EDITORIAL CARTOONIST:
SCRITCH! SCRITCH!
SCRITCH! SCRITCH!
11-11-91

Well?
Eddie Arnold!
John Sununu!
M.C. Hammer!

How about **this**?
William Buckley!
Rich Little!
Calvin Coolidge!
© PHIL (HERE'S INK IN YOUR EYE.) FRANK

This?
Willie Brown!
The Righteous Brothers!
Having a bit of trouble doing Frank Jordan.

IT'S THANKSGIVING AND **FARLEY'S** DISHING DINNER AT **ST. ANTHONY'S**:
Nice of you to come down to do this, Farley..

Well... I didn't really have any place to go this year.. I don't have any **real** family myself. My friends are all with their parents and children...
And I'm not seeing Irene anymore...

11-28-91
My bird won't allow me to cook a turkey in the apartment. It's against his religion..
I guess I could've gone to McDonald's..
© PHIL (BLESSED ARE THE HUMBLE PIES) FRANK

Farley.. **please**.. you're depressing our clientele.
Get some air. Take the dessert cart for a spin around the parking lot.

12-10-91

©Phil (TO SLEEP, PERCHANCE TO DREAM) Frank

12-18-91

©Phil (BEAT ME UP, SCOTTY!) Frank

1-3-92

©Phil (NAME THAT TUNA!) Frank

I see.. the rangers.. ..they have joined hands.. ..they are singing..

GIVE FEES A CHANCE..

Lost Horizons is a combination bar and laundromat. I've always pictured it as a place where bachelors bond over beer while doing their laundry.

Joe the bartender is modeled on my long-time writing pal and fellow car buff, Joe Troise. Farley doesn't go to Lost Horizons often but then he doesn't do his laundry often, either.

In this series you'll witness the birth of a new cartoon character, **Orwell T. Catt**. The "T" stands for "The". The disappearance of songbirds in general and in Golden Gate Park specifically was being blamed on the feral cat population.

The cat lovers said the cause was environmental, not feline. The City Parks Commission was holding hearings. My first thought was to put a cat or two on the witness stand.

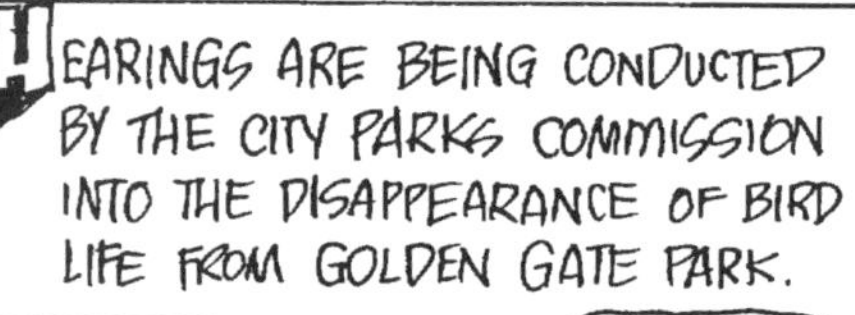

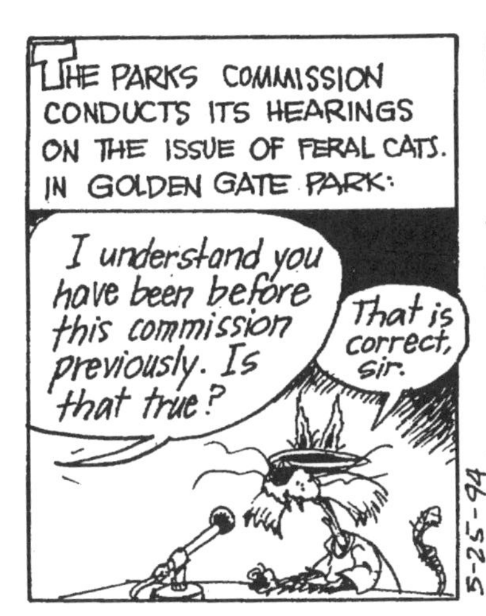
THE PARKS COMMISSION CONDUCTS ITS HEARINGS ON THE ISSUE OF FERAL CATS IN GOLDEN GATE PARK:
I understand you have been before this commission previously. Is that true?
That is correct, sir.
5-25-94

Do you acknowledge that the feral cats are decimating our songbird population, Mr. Orwell?
I can only speak for myself, commissioner, when I say that while I may have had lust in my heart, I never raised a claw with the...

BRING IN THE WITNESS!
© Phil (I ONLY WINGED HIM) Frank
I'm dead meat.

A RUSH OF EXCITEMENT RIPPLES THROUGH THE AUDIENCE AS A WITNESS COMES FORWARD AT THE PARKS COMMISSION HEARINGS:
5-26-94
State your name please.
My name is Ken. I'm a killdeer.

You are aware that the purpose of this hearing is to take testimony about the effect the presence of feral cats in Golden Gate Park is having on the bird population.
Yes, sir.

© Phil (PORK LIPS NOW) Frank
Tell us about your injured wing.
Well, Mister Commissioner, on the morning of May the...
OBJECTION!
Any ornithologist will tell you that the "crippled wing" ploy is merely a distraction display!
This guy's a genius...

IN THE HALLWAY OUTSIDE THE OFFICES OF THE CITY'S PARKS AND RECREATION DEPARTMENT ORWELL AND HIS ATTORNEY CONFER:
LOOK! YOU FERAL CATS ARE IN A BAD SITUATION!!
SCRATCH!
FERAL
5-27-94

THE BIRD POPULATION IS DWINDLING, DUDE! YOU'VE GOT A PUBLIC RELATIONS DISASTER ON YOUR PAWS, MAN!

It's time to cut your losses! Plead guilty to a lesser offense! Throw yourself on the mercy of the Parks Commission!!
SCRATCH!
SCRATCH!
SCRATCH
SCRATCH
FERAL AND PRUNED
© Phil (THE 5 TO 7 YEAR ITCH) Frank
This is what's known in the legal profession as flea-bargaining.
Are YOU listening, dude?
SCRITCH!
SCRATCH!
FERAL AND PRUNED

When Farley arrived in San Francisco in 1986, I moved him into a third-floor flat in North Beach. I imagined that over the years he'd move from neighborhood to neighborhood in the city.

I liked North Beach so much that I kept him there for seven years. With the push to develop lofts in the SoMa area, I decided to move the guy and his bird. No complaints from them yet.

It's not that I don't like the loft concept.. It's quite exciting, miss..
Call me Xenia.

3-7-92
Xenia! See.. I live in an ancient North Beach flat.. ..maybe 800 square feet.. 10-foot ceilings.. This amount of space is.. well.. overwhelming...
I see..

And everyone I see around here is so... um.. hip looking. Where I'm living is more 'old world'..
It's okay... I understand.. Here. Maybe this'll help.
©Phil (I'LL HAVE THE WORKS!) Frank
Dr. Hilarita Potter.. Lifestyles Adjustment Specialist and Ear piercing.
Good luck.

IN ONE BOLD MOVE FARLEY MAKES A MAJOR LIFESTYLE CHANGE:
NOW LEAVING NORTH BEACH. YOU'LL REGRET IT!
Cafe
HE ABANDONS THE COZY NORTH BEACH VICTORIAN FLAT HE HAS OCCUPIED FOR SEVEN YEARS...
3-9-92

...AND RELOCATES HIS DOMICILE TO A SOUTH-OF-MARKET ARTIST'S LOFT.
I can fly! I can fly!!

HE SIMULTANEOUSLY ABANDONS HIS DROUGHT-AND-BACHELOR-RESISTANT CACTUS FOR A 15-FOOT-TALL FICUS.
My own tree! Really! You shouldn't have!!

..AND VACATES HIS DESK AT THE DAILY REQUIREMENT TO CREATE A WORK SPACE IN HIS WAREHOUSE HOME:
Look, Marian!! stove.. washer... dryer.. answering machine.. FAX.. word processor..
©Phil (SURREAL LIFE GUY) Frank
And how was your first day in a live/work situation?
Great.. except I faxed my underwear to the paper.

FARLEY IS VERGING ON GIDDINESS OVER HIS NEW SOUTH-OF-MARKET DIGS:
?
COME ON, BRUCE!! CATCH ME IF YOU CAN!

3-10-92
THE SWITCH FROM CROWDED FLAT TO SPACIOUS ARTIST'S LOFT MAY BE TOO MUCH FOR OUR RESERVED WORDSMITH.
WHEEEEE!
I think he's losing it.

You know, Farley... there are certain emotional disorders that stem from sudden lifestyle changes.
I know..
©Phil (A TALE OF TWO PSYCHES) Frank

I'm suffering from an "edifice complex" Ha.. ha.. ha.. ha...
He's definitely losing it!

Our mayor, Frank Jordan, was making some very strange appointments to city positions. My friend John McCosker was preparing to retire from his position as director of the Steinhart Aquarium. I pictured Frank appointing Orwell T. Catt to the vacated position. After all, who's more interested in fish than a cat?

It's true I carried Frank's flyers to every doorstep in the outer Richmond and did unspeakable things to every Agnos sign in the Haight!

FERAL AND PROUD

But there are a dozen sound reasons for my appointment as head of the Aquarium. My qualifications speak for themselves!!

Name one.

© Phil (SICK TRANSIT.) Frank

Construction had begun on the New Main Library, and who would be more excited about such an undertaking than one of the city's librarians? Enter Marian - seldom seen in the strip but recognized as the "other woman" in our bachelor's life. Farley turns to Marian, in the reference section of his local branch, when his little bachelor brain needs information on relationships.

The mayor was still having his problems. He was rousting the street people from their homeless camps–one of his campaign promises. He wasn't getting a lot of good press for his efforts.

I was listening to a radio report about Jordan's idea to create homeless vans intended to help the street people with needs. When I first heard the report on the radio I could've sworn that the announcer said "homeless fans".

The tensions of daily life in San Francisco and the pressures of running a restaurant start to get to our urbanized bears.

They decide to take a break and return to their roots – Asphalt State Park. Sooo... they call a taxi.

IN THE OFFICE OF THE FOG CITY DUMPSTER:
Hilda... I'm worried about Alphonse..
Why?
6-23-92

I think he needs a vacation... to get out to the woods.. He's not himself.
What's he doing?

He's very tense and ill-tempered. In fact.. I've seen him badgering customers..
Sweet Alphonse.. ..badgering the customers?
©Phil Frank (SUSHI SELF)
See for yourself.
SO!! The salmon's not fresh, is it? How about some nice fresh badger? Huh?
GRRRRR

AT THE WEEKLY EMPLOYEES' MEETING AT THE DUMPSTER:
Alphonse has the floor!!
I don't know about the rest of you, but I'd like to go back to the woods.
QUIT?
6-24-92

No. Just take a vacation. We could all go back to Asphalt State Park for a month.
But.. could we handle the shock of being back in nature.

Well... they do have a 24-hour market, a video parlor and a morning paper delivery...
Tempting.
Any new conveniences?

©Phil Frank (WHEN IN DOUBT... PUTT.)
They just opened a pitch & putt miniature golf course. Vice-President Quayle threw out the first ball!!
Call a taxi!

WITH A BACKUP CREW OF FOUR DOGS AND A RACCOON IN CHARGE OF THE EATERY, THE BEARS TAKE THEIR LEAVE:
Remember.. NO credit cards!
6-25-92

Looks like you folks are going on vacation. Am I taking you to the airport?
FOG CITY
TAXI
ONE NEAT CITY

Here's a map. We're going there. Asphalt State Park.
Oh?
©Phil Frank (CLOTHED FOR THE HOLIDAYS)

Dispatch! This is 47. I've got four fares. I'm en route to Asphalt State Park via my apartment to get my swim trunks.
Back in a few days. Over.

HORACE MALONE'S RINGING PHONE WAKENS HIM FROM A DREAM IN WHICH HE IS BEING GIVEN AN AWARD FOR THE PLUSHEST OFFICE IN THE PARK SYSTEM:
ZZZZZZZZ
RING!
HEAD RANGER
6-29-92

Ranger Malone.. Sorry to disturb you, sir. It's Cogswell at the entrance kiosk.
Sir.. do we charge for the car if it's just dropping off campers?
A taxicab, sir.
TAXI
STOP

Okay.. No charge to enter but $5 to turn around..
Second question.. ..what is the day use charge for bears?
©Phil (QUEASY RIDER) Frank
WE LIVE HERE, DUDE!!
Sorry, sir... ..I didn't hear that.. No bears allowed?

THE CAB DRIVER APPEARS TO BE ANXIOUS TO LEAVE HIS FARES AT THE PARK.
Here's your receipt. Save it for when you leave.
Hope you enjoyed your visit!
STOP
SCREEEE
6-30-92

See.. I don't make the rules here.. I just enforce them. The Head Ranger says no bears are allowed in the park.

How would you like to have a real wilderness experience?
©Phil (YOUR SPACE OR MINE?) Frank
Campsite C-13? Hey! That's right next to the video rental!!
Theyre back..

THROUGH THEIR NATURAL CUNNING AND CONVERSATIONAL SKILLS, THE BEARS HAVE TALKED THEIR WAY INTO ASPHALT STATE PARK:
Ahh.. smell that air!
Chili dogs!! ..or my mother didn't own a fur coat!
YOO HOO!!
7-3-92

Glad I caught you... Listen.. Ranger Malone would have a fit if he found out I let you into the park.. so here are some V.I.P. badges that you..

BADGES??
Oh Oh.
Yes.. you just pin this on and if you see a ranger..
V.I.P.
©Phil (WHEN YOU CARE ENOUGH TO SEND THE VERY BEAST)
I DON'T GOT TO SHOW YOU NO..
Thank you, ranger. Here's some honey-comb for all your trouble.

SHOPPERS AT THE ASPHALT STATE PARK SUPERMARKET ARE STARTLED WHEN A BEAR ENTERS THE STORE:
AEIII!!
BEAR!!

Excuse me .. the sign in the window says you have bear-proof food containers..
Y..Y.. yes..we do. They rent for th.. th.. three dollars a d..d..day..
7-9-92

See? They're made of extruded p..p..plastic and are impossible for b..b..b..bears to crush or open unless they know how..
Good. I want to rent one for a month.

B..b..but you're a bear!!
Yes and I'm traveling with three other bears I want to keep out of my food!
© Phil (THE PILLAGE BLACKSMITH) Frank

MRS. MELMAC HAS THE FOREST FLOOR AT A WOODSY GATHERING:
ASPHALT STATE PARK
ONE NEAT PARK!
ARE YOU WITH ME, CAMPERS?
YES!!
YES!!

We can collect every twig, needle, leaf, acorn and pine cone but that will only rid us of nature's litter. The problem goes deeper!!
Tell us, sister!!
7-10-92

The problem is that down under it all is DIRT!! D..I..R..T...!! Now the park has done great work! They've paved the roads and the parking spots!! And they've put in curbs!
YES!! CURB THE WILDERNESS!
© Phil (TRADE) MARK TRAIL) Frank
But what we must work for and strive for and fight for is...
Tell us!!
Congoleum on the nature trails!!
YES!!!

USING HER PATENTED "NATURE BEATER" VACUUM AND A 1500-FOOT EXTENSION CORD, MRS. MELMAC WORKS HER WAY ALONG A LEAF-COVERED NATURE TRAIL:
WHRRRRRRR
Uh... Mrs. Melmac..

7-11-92
The management of Asphalt State Park certainly appreciates your "ONE NEAT PARK" campaign to remove litter from the grounds..
RRRRR

..But leaves, twigs, acorns and needles are important parts of the compost from which new life springs and by which nature replenishes and feeds her..
SEE THIS TATTOO?
© Phil (UNTIL DIRT DO US PART) Frank

"DEATH TO DIRT!"
I'll be in my kiosk if you need me.

Bruce D. Raven, in a major political misjudgment, throws his support behind a bird named **H. Ross Parrot**. Not long thereafter, Sesame Street featured a character of the same name and look as mine! My copyright instincts aroused, I conferred with Chronicle attorneys. We filed notices! We pounded our chests! Then we dropped the whole thing. Who wants to be remembered as the guys who sued the Children's Television Network?

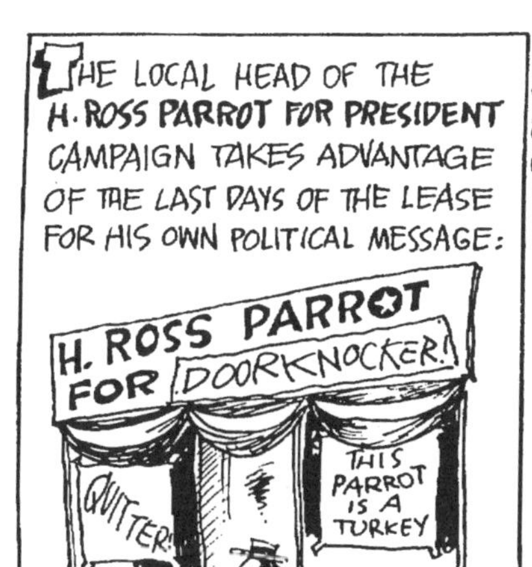
THE LOCAL HEAD OF THE H. ROSS PARROT FOR PRESIDENT CAMPAIGN TAKES ADVANTAGE OF THE LAST DAYS OF THE LEASE FOR HIS OWN POLITICAL MESSAGE:
H. ROSS PARROT FOR DOORKNOCKER!
QUITTER
THIS PARROT IS A TURKEY
7-27-92

I've been hornswoggled, bamboozled, hoaxed and humbugged!!
PARRO

I've been led up the garden path and down the primrose path!! I've been handed a bill of goods... fed a line.. given a bum steer!!
© Phil (REBEL WITH A CAW.) Frank

I'm so angry I could just molt!!
Come home, Bruce.

THE FORMER CAMPAIGN DIRECTOR'S HARANGUE CONTINUES:
That lily-livered lyin' little relative of the cuckoo!! ..That pea-brained, yellow-bellied, sap-sucking..
H. ROSS PARROT FOR DOORKNOCKER!
QUITTER
THIS PARROT IS A TURKEY
7-28-92

A BLACK STRETCH LIMO WITH TEXAS PLATES GLIDES TO THE CURB. A TINTED WINDOW IS LOWERED:
Bzzzzzz
That... ..that.. that.

IT'S H. ROSS PARROT!
Ah admahr your forthrightness. Would ya'all be in charge of mah "Take Back America" home shopper's network?
Sure! I'll do that. Anything you say, sir.

We'll be in touch.
Swell!! I'll wait right here until I hear from you, chief. 'Bye.
© Phil (A LITTLE SLIGHT OF MIND.) Frank
Am I a sucker or what?

CITIZEN IRE HAS REACHED A FEVER PITCH OVER PERKS IN THE FORM OF LUXURY CARS FOR CITY STAFF:
There'll be some changes around here! Write this down...

"STAFF WILL BE ALLOWED TO DRIVE CITY-OWNED VEHICLES HOME BUT WILL HAVE TO CARRY FARES."
DALY CITY! ANYONE WANT TO GO TO DALY CITY?
SAN FRANCISCO CITY TAXI
10-16-92

"ALL LUXURY CARS WILL BE RETURNED FOR STRIPPED-DOWN MODELS":
Satisfied?
MUNI SUPERVISOR
© Phil (THERE'S A FORDABLE IN YOUR FUTURE) Frank

"CARS WHOSE VALUE IS LESS THAN THE COST OF HOUSING A DESTITUTE INDIVIDUAL WILL BE GIVEN AWAY":
The tank's full. Here are the keys and a map of Oregon.

The San Francisco Board of Supervisors is considering a radical move... to require MUNI officials to not only give up their city-owned cars but to ride to work on their own transit system...
NEW
10-30-92
SOME TRAINING REQUIRED
WHAT?? R..R..Ride in a **bus** with the p..p..public?
Have you **seen** those vehicles? They're a mess!!
This could be considered cruel and unusual punishment!
There's **got** to be a way around this...
I'VE GOT IT!
Okay.. let's say I ride a Muni electric train..
Can I attach a private car?

YAWN!
Time to hibernate again. As far as I know, these four bears are the only characters in the cartoon world to drop out of sight for a portion of the year.
This precedent-setting quartet then reappears each spring, just in time for the Giants' home opener.
INCOMING!

DEEP WITHIN THE HIBERNATION DEN, **HILDA**, THE MATRIARCH OF THE BEAR CLAN, HAS FINALLY GOTTEN EVERYONE INSIDE:
FOG CITY DUMPSTER
CLOSED FOR HIBERNATION
Is everyone settled?
Yep.
I guess.
Yes.
11-13-92
Okay.. I'm going to set the alarm for April and turn out the light..
Okay..
YAWNNN..
'Night
Do you think Angela Alioto will orchestrate a takeover of the palace? What do you think Hillary will wear to the Inaugural Ball?
LET'S HYBERNATE!
Do you think Pat Robertson will go to Camp David for a visit and never be seen again?
Did you clean out the coffee machine?
Yep. I drank it all..
Oh, **great**!
Do you think..

Orwell T. Catt, out of work since all the brook trout disappeared from the Steinhart Aquarium fish tanks, is elated when opportunity scratches at the door asking to be let in.

He's named head of security for the soon-to-be First Cat "Socks."

11-24-92

INFURIATED BY THE PRESS USING CATNIP TO LURE HIS FAMILY'S PET CAT "**SOCKS**" OUTSIDE THE GROUNDS OF THE ARKANSAS STATE GOVERNOR'S MANSION, CLINTON HAS TAKEN DIRECT ACTION:

RRRRRRRRRRR

THE NEW BODYGUARD FOR THE CLINTON'S CAT EXPLAINS THE WORLD TO HIS CHARGE:
11-25-92
Okay "Socks"... now listen up!
FERAL AND

First of all... Don't trust the press! They'll only use you. No photo ops unless I'm around. No quotes either. Just stonewall 'em!
FERAL AND PROUD

See.. you've been a pretty pampered pussycat. Me, I've been out on the streets surviving. That's why they brought me in... so always look to me for direction..
© Phil (GOD TO THE LAST CROP.) Frank

And if any newshound lures you again with catnip... give it to me for.. er.. testing!!

Dateline: Little Rock
WITH HIS SUNGLASSES ON AND HIS LISTENING DEVICE IN PLACE, ORWELL, OFFICIAL BODYGUARD TO "SOCKS," SCANS THE PRESS CONFERENCE:
12-10-92

CLINTON'S ORDER TO THE PRESS WAS CLEAR: STAY AWAY FROM THEIR CAT!
I could sure use a scoop.
FERAL AND PROUD

There's one in the corner.
You're right!! It's Socks' kitty litter scoop. Hee. Hee!... I'll just..
© Phil (SCOOP DU JOUR) Frank

AN HOUR LATER.. AT A LOCAL HOSPITAL'S EMERGENCY ROOM:
Remember that scene in Aliens? How'd they get the thing off the guy's face?

THE CLINTONS ARE HOSTING A HOLIDAY OPEN HOUSE AT THE ARKANSAS GOVERNOR'S MANSION:
12-24-92
Okay, Socks... Listen up! This is your first official public event.

I'll be watching you constantly. You can move around the room with the security of knowing your bodyguard has his eyes on you at every moment!!

I'll be standing over there monitoring your every move from the vicinity of the buffet table... in the area of those seafood appetizers...
FERAL AND PROUD
© Phil (SALMON CHANTED EVENING) Frank

Specifically there, where he's placing that smoked salmon.
Just scream if you need help.

"He will be found comatose two weeks later in a notorious sardine oil den in Marseilles!"

OUR FLOUNDER

SACRÉ BLEU!!

Every year about this time, when the rains come to the Bay Area, they soak and soften the red berries of the pyracantha bushes and the birds proceed to indulge themselves on the fermenting berries. They get... well... a little loopy. Common symptoms are flying into windows and falling out of trees.

RAIN... RAIN... RAIN... Seemed like it would never stop back in January 1993.

News reports on television kept showing rivers overflowing their banks and people's basements flooding.

I thought "basements" and then I thought of the bears in their underground den beneath the **Fog City Dumpster**.

Let's see if you enjoy bungee jumping, Socks...

Orwell's career has moved into high gear now that he has accompanied the Clinton clan to Washington, D.C. and the White House Here in the capitol, Orwell is the head of Feline Security and, as such, is in charge of the First Cat's well-being. Poor **Socks**!

This is base commander to all units. I am taking "Hairball" out for his walk. Any snickering on this frequency will result in immediate dismissal! over.

PLACES EVERYONE!!

Poor Frank Jordan. Every time the mayor turned around, someone in city government was throwing a wrench in the works. Supervisor Bill Maher got in a yelling match with the police chief Tony Ribera about Bill's girlfriend Joanne Welch's job. Angela Alioto, head of the Board of Supervisors, was out to get his goat, his job **and** his panda bear.

What a town!

THE ANNOUNCEMENT THAT SUPERVISOR BILL MAHER REGRETS HIS RECENT 'POOR JUDGMENT' SENT SHOCK WAVES THROUGH SAN FRANCISCO CITY HALL...
WHODOA!!
6.2 on the Richter Scale!!

2-27-93
..BUT THE NEWS THAT THE POLITICAL SOAP OPERA MIGHT SOON BE COMING TO AN END WAS EVEN MORE SHOCKING TO THE CITY'S THEATER COMMUNITY..
CASTING CALL

..WHERE THREE DIFFERENT PRODUCTIONS ARE CURRENTLY IN THE WORKS:
"THE CRASS MENAGERIE"
THE INSIDE STORY of SAN FRANCISCO CITY HALL
OPENING SOON!
The show must go on!
CASTING CALL
© PHIL (PLACES, EVERYONE!!) Frank

REHEARSALS FOR THE THEATRICAL FARCE "THE CRASS MENAGERIE" CONTINUE AT THE CURRENT THEATER:
Okay... siblings at the table. Frank standing stage left..

I leave town on business and your mother calls me every day about your antics.. Backbiting, sexual harassment charges, press conferences, fistfights!!
Every day a new problem! SHAME ON YOU!!
3-2-93

At this point, the morning paper arrives, stage left.. The patient father retrieves it and reads the headlines...
He will move to center stage..
THUD!
© PHIL (WHO WRITES THEIR MATERIAL??) Frank
Where he will... ..GOOD LORD!!
SCRIPT CHANGE!!

"THE CRASS MENAGERIE" REHEARSALS CONTINUE AT THE CURRENT THEATER:
In this scene the entire family is gathered in the living room...

FRANK SPEAKS..
Billy!! Stop hitting Terence!
JOANNE!! STOP POINTING YOUR FINGER AT TONY!!
Tony!! Put that gun down! It's not a toy!
Angela!! You're going to put someone's eye out with that gavel!!
3-3-93

At this point Frank picks up his goddaughter and puts her on his knee..
Then he speaks..
© PHIL (IS THERE AN ATTORNEY IN THE HOUSE?)
You, alone, behaved yourself while I was gone, Annemarie...
How would you like to be head of the Public Utilities Commission?
WAAAA!!

ACRES OF ASPHALT, CABLE TV HOOKUPS, A "CURB THE WILDERNESS" PAVING PROJECT AND ONE MAN IN CHARGE: **HORACE MALONE**. WHEN THE STRIP WAS SYNDICATED NATIONALLY, FARLEY WAS A SEASONAL RANGER AT THE PARK AND MALONE WAS HIS BOSS. THEY STILL STAY IN TOUCH. WHEN THESE STRIPS RAN, CALIFORNIA LEGISLATORS WERE CUTTING PARK BUDGETS AND EVEN ELIMINATING MANY PARKS.

HORACE MALONE, HEAD RANGER FROM ASPHALT STATE PARK, IS BEING GRILLED BY A COST-CUTTING TASK FORCE OF STATE PARK EXECUTIVES:
How do you justify a $300,000 expenditure to cement the nature trails?
It was part of our "Pave the Wilderness" program.
3-9-93

MEANWHILE, BACK AT THE PARK, AN AIR OF APPREHENSION PREVAILS:
What if they do close the park? How will we get our snack foods... our peanut butter?
We'll have to forage in the woods.

NOT ME, DUDE!! I'll do anything before I'll eat berries and nuts and grubs again!!
© Phil (BACK TO THE FORAGE-ERATOR) Frank

WILL FIZH FOR FOOD!!
Fish are food, you idiot!

AT THE STATE PARK BUDGET HEARINGS:
Horace Malone... it is the opinion of this committee that Asphalt State Park is the most inefficiently run park in our system!!
Gulp!
5-10-93

But it is also our opinion that to close the park would be a disservice to the public...we will allow you, if major cutbacks are made, to remain open...
YOU WILL?

A THOUSAND BLESSINGS UPON YOU AND YOUR DESCENDANTS! YOU WILL NOT REGRET THIS... CUTBACKS, YES!! SALARIES, EQUIPMENT... OVERTIME.... THANK YOU... THANK YOU!!
© Phil (THE PALL OF THE WILD) Frank
RANGER STERN GROVE? THIS IS MALONE... FIRE THE BEARS!!

THOUSANDS OF FORMS FLUTTER DOWN FROM THE ASPHALT STATE PARK HELICOPTER TO THE FOREST FAR BELOW...
WHUPPA WHUPPA

6-12-93
WHAT IS THIS.. ACID RAIN?
Worse! They appear to be rental agreements..

"Due to extensive cutbacks in state park funding, it will be necessary to begin charging animals who live in the woods day-use fees. Please pay at the ranger station."
Ranger Horace Malone
© Phil (WOODEN YOU KNOW IT!) Frank

Pay? To live in the woods?
Welcome to the '90s.

Oh, woe was Bill Clinton. His first 100 days had been rough. He needed help! Orwell T. Catt could provide that help by going under the knife. Readers were convinced that I wouldn't actually have Orwell neutered.

I'm fairly certain he is the first cartoon character in the history of the comic strip to go under the X-Acto knife.

If you **don't** agree to my proposal I'll personally perform the operation on you without anethesia and put you on cockroach patrol in the basement of the Treasury Building for the next four years!

Well... that answers that.

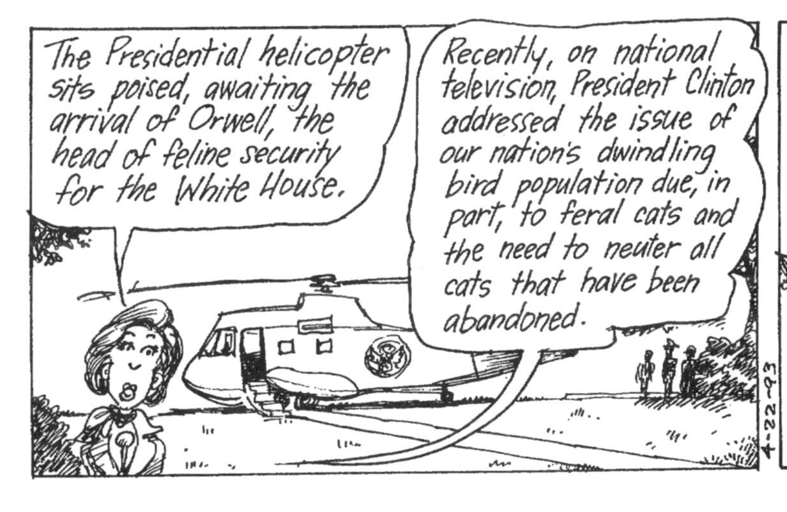

IN THE OPERATING ROOM OF THE SAN FRANCISCO S.P.C.A.:
President Clinton is on the phone.
4-27-93

Orwell... It's Bill. I hope you can hear me. All Americans are proud of you as you make this sacrifice for the good of our future bird population.

Feral cats **must** be neutered if we are to protect our songbirds. I am proud of you and consider you a true patriot! Good luck!
Gulp!
© Phil (ONE IF BY LAND, TWO IF BY SEA) Frank

To paraphrase another great patriot, **Nathan Hale**..." I only regret that I have but two"... ...uh... Oh, never mind!
PREPARE THE ANESTHESIA!

PRESIDENT CLINTON'S HEAD OF FELINE SECURITY ADDRESSES THE LEGISLATURE IN SACRAMENTO:
Ladies and gentlemen. Perhaps you are wondering why a feral cat in a hospital gown is addressing you today...

Bill Clinton asked me to help the nation and its bird population by volunteering to be neutered. Yesterday I took that step.
4-28-93

You will soon be reviewing Assembly Bill 302, which, with some amendments, will encourage the neutering of feral cats and, in turn, help save our bird population. Bill and I urge your support!
© Phil (FOR BETTER OR WORSE) Frank

I feel like such a turncat!
CLAP!! CLAP!! CLAP!
CLAP!! CLAP!!
CLAP!! CLAP!!

SYMPATHY RUNS HIGH AMONG THE MAINLY MALE MEMBERS OF THE WHITE HOUSE SECRET SERVICE UNIT FOR THE RECENTLY NEUTERED HEAD OF FELINE SECURITY:
Tough luck...
You said it. Boy, I'd...
Shh! Here he comes!

Orwell... I'd like to present you with a get-well gift on behalf of the guys...
That's nice.
FERAL AND PROUD
5-11-93

© Phil (THE GOOD, THE BAD AND THE SCRAGGLY) Frank
You fellas are really a swell bunch...
And you have a really sick sense of humor!
FERAL AND PRUNED.

STILL RECOVERING FROM HIS NEUTERING OPERATION, ORWELL, THE FERAL CAT, LOUNGES IN THE ROSE GARDEN. HE IS A CHANGED CAT:
This is one of my favorite poems. It's by A.E. Housman.

"With rue my heart is laden
For laughing friends I had,
For many a rose-lipt maiden
And many a light-foot lad.
By brooks too broad for leaping
The light-foot lads are laid
And rose-lipt girls are sleeping
In fields where roses fade."
5-12-93

It speaks to me of a life spent... of loves lost and the death of desire. My own, I suspect.
Sniffle
©Phil (I NEVER PROMISED YOU A PROSE GARDEN) Frank
You heard me! Get a tranquilizer gun and a vial of testosterone to the Oval Office... NOW!

IN AN ATTEMPT TO RE-ESTABLISH THE VIRILITY OF THE NEUTERED HEAD OF FELINE SECURITY FOR THE WHITE HOUSE, CLINTON TAKES A RADICAL STEP:
Aim for his haunch, Mr. President. The testosterone will do the rest.
Okay. I'll take it from here.

This next poem is by Alexander Pope and speaks of nature and the universal good.
BLAM!

THWAP!
FERAL AND PRUNED
5-13-93

©Phil (CONAN THE THESPIAN) Frank
I wonder if there're any poems in here by Arnold Schwarzenegger.
I'm outta here...

AS THE MORNING SUNLIGHT FILTERS INTO THE OVAL OFFICE, BILL CLINTON SIPS HIS COFFEE AND PONDERS HIS POLITICAL FUTURE:
I've really got to start making better decisions...
6-7-93

One of these days I'll be picking a Supreme Court nominee. If only there were an androgynous, celibate individual who wouldn't offend anyone...

Hmm...
FERAL AND PRUNED
©Phil (ONCE MORE, WITH FELINES) Frank
Get a grip on yourself, Bill !!

With Farley's Chrysler Rebate loaded to the gunnels with camping gear, the nuclear family of Farley, Irene, Olive and Bruce the raven head for the woods to escape the urban scene and do a little tree hugging.

OUR VACATIONING URBANITES GET THEIR FIRST GLIMPSE OF THE NORTHWEST WILDERNESS:
LOOK!! A GROVE OF GIANT SEQUOIAS! WHAT MAJESTY!

MOM... FARLEY... LOOK! AN ELK! WOW! I'VE ONLY SEEN THEM ON TV!
OOO! OOO!
7-7-93

What do you see that's so exciting, Bruce?
© Paul (ONLY TWO PIECES OF CARRION...) Frank
Roadkill.
Sorry I asked.

AT LAIDBACK STATE PARK SOMEWHERE IN THE NORTHWEST:
AHHH!! SMELL THIS AIR!!
7-8-93

It's just us and the wilderness! Not a single urban intrusion to spoil our communion with nature!!
All in favor of a wildflower walk raise your..
KNOCK!! KNOCK!!

KNOCK... KNOCK?
Hi. I work in the lumber industry. President Clinton has drafted a logging plan that would put many of us out of work...
© Paul (SIGN ON THE DOTTED LION) Frank

I have this petition...
Ohhhh...
I'll come back some other time.

AT LAIDBACK STATE PARK IN THE PACIFIC NORTHWEST:
FARLEY!! BRUCE IS GONE!
That's okay, Olive... He's a bird. He's out meeting friends, no doubt.

So you're a Spotted Owl? So this is what all the squabbling's about?!
I'm afraid so...
7-10-93

It's rather embarrassing really. We weren't looking for all this attention. We're just trying to live where we've always lived.
© Paul (WHO GIVES A HOOT) Frank

I thought Ted Koppel was a little rough on you on Nightline.
Well... I've got an agent now.

Precious Foods. I just couldn't resist a little needling of the health food markets... especially the upscale ones. The food is wonderful, but when I visited a couple of stores, my "pretentiousness alarm" kept going off.

BABA "RELATES" TO A CUSTOMER AT PRECIOUS FOODS.
I'm interested in this Casaba melon.
A fine choice, madam. That one is my particular favorite.
7-30-93
Is it organic?
It is organic, fat-free, non-toxic, unbleached and biodegradable!! It was raised in a non-violent household in the clean air of the Andean foothills.
It was flown in fresh just this morning.
How much is it?
$324.00
That's a lot for a Casaba melon.
We can only fit four in a seat. Why, the airfare alone...
© Phil (Was it a movie flight?) Frank
I'll take it if its papers are in order.
We'll just have them notarized.
RAOUL!!

INSIDE "PRECIOUS FOODS":
Mister Re Bok... could you direct me to your "special cereal"?
All my cereals are special ma'am...
7-31-93
All are made from organically-grown, unbleached grain... fat and sodium free. Expensive, but worth almost every penny..
I want the "special" cereal you sell only to members of MENSA. My card.
Aha! I'll get some from the back room.
© Phil (No two flakes alike!) Frank
REASON BRAN! Clears your head and your lower digestive tract!!
NUTS TO YOU!
NUTRA WHEAT
WHOLE GRAIN
GOOD EARTH
REASON BRAN
FIRST FIBER
TRUE GRIT CEREAL
GRAINY TRAIN

THE CAMPERS RETURN:
Hey, Farley... Check it out... Baba's doing an ad on TV!
WHAT?
WE AT PRECIOUS FOODS MARKET ARE HERE TO SERVE...
8-4-93
"PRECIOUS FOODS"?
The freshest, most exotic and, coincidentally, expensive foods are available for purchase...
Or... if you're having a dinner party and want to impress your friends with a few $20 heads of arugula around the kitchen...
© Phil (Lettuce pray...) Frank
Don't buy it. Lease it! By the day... only through Precious Foods. Our FAX number is 415 332-9197!
Oh, nooo...
Boy! Leave town for a week...

When readers question how I come up with some of this wacky material, I always mention Officer Bob Geary, a ventriloquist, and his puppet, Brendan O'Smarty. The chief of police told officer Geary he couldn't drive around with the puppet in the car. Officer Geary got enough signatures to get the issue on the ballot as Prop BB. It passed by a big margin.

I voted for Prop BB, the police puppet issue.
Really?
11-2-93

You weren't concerned that the decision-making process would be in the hands of the patrolman rather than his superiors?
No.

I knew what would happen if puppets are outlawed!
Ahh...
©Phil (WOODEN YOU KNOW IT!) Frank
ONLY OUTLAWS WILL HAVE PUPPETS!!

THE ISSUE OF PROP BB, THE POLICE PUPPET, HAS SPAWNED A SPINOFF:
This is a stick-up! Give me all your cash!
S..S...SURE THING!

It's an interesting legal ploy in the event you get caught... that the puppet pulled off the robbery... but you'll never get away with it.
11-3-93

Yeah? Why?
Because I could see your lips move.
©Phil (LOOSE LIPS SINK QUIPS) Frank

Haven't you ever heard the old adage about never insulting a ventriloquist who's got a gun?
I have now!

AN UNUSUAL ROBBERY IS UNDER WAY IN THE CITY:
PUT A CARTON OF CAMELS IN WITH THE CASH...

SURE THING... ...ANYTHING ELSE?
11-4-93

ATTENTION, ALL UNITS! A 214 IN PROGRESS AT 155 SANSOME.
214?

That's a robbery involving a puppet!!
3 ADAM 12 RESPONDING!!
RRRA
©Phil (DON'T BE A SAP.) Frank

Hang on, Brendan! This could be your shining hour!!
I never knew a puppet could sweat.

A BLACK-AND-WHITE SCREECHES TO A HALT OUTSIDE A GROCERY WHERE A 214 IS IN PROGRESS:
GROCE
RRRRRRRRR

A 214 IS A ROBBERY INVOLVING A PUPPET:
POLICE! FREEZE!! DROP THE GUN OR YOU'RE SAWDUST!
The jig's up!

Okay, copper... you got us. But this wasn't **my** idea! **He** made me do it. He used me!!
Why, you...
11-5-93
©Phil (WOULD YOU BELIEVE NAUGHTY PINE?) Frank

You have the right to remain silent. Anything you say...
You'd better hope we get separate cells, you fir-fabricated fink!!
Gulp.

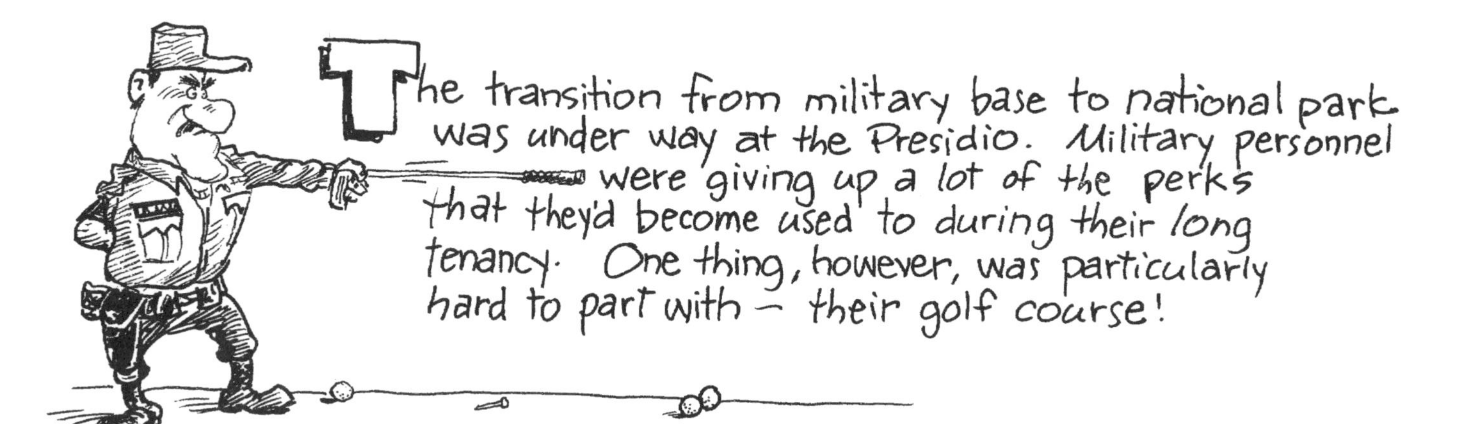
The transition from military base to national park was under way at the Presidio. Military personnel were giving up a lot of the perks that they'd become used to during their long tenancy. One thing, however, was particularly hard to part with – their golf course!

OUT AT THE PRESIDIO:
Gentlemen... the briefing will now commence!
You have volunteered for a very dangerous mission.
1-12-94

On Sunday, January 16, at 0800 hours we will commence the operation. Our goal is to take and hold the **Presidio Golf Course!**
GASP

The Sierra Club Task Force and the Park Service want this little plum. Well, soldiers, they'll have to **fight** for it!!
©Phil (GOLF WAR) Frank

Sir! Does this mission have a name?
From now on, son, you are a part of Operation Divot Storm!

PREPARATIONS FOR OPERATION DIVOT STORM ARE UNDER WAY AT THE PRESIDIO:
Gentlemen.. It is our mission to take and hold the Presidio Golf Course!
1-13-94

This operation will require precise timing, coordination and, above all, surprise! To further that aim each of you will be issued a complete set of camouflage...

Send out Corporal Zawicki!
©Phil (TURN THE OTHER CHIC!) Frank
Each outfit will consist of a golf cap, a blue Ban-Lon shirt, green golf sweater, yellow slacks with a red and pink plaid pattern, tassled white golf shoes and an M-16.

PLANS FOR OPERATION DIVOT STORM ARE UNDER WAY:

Gentlemen... I will put it to you bluntly... when we attempt to capture the Presidio Golf Course on Sunday we will be greatly outnumbered!

To better our odds against the Sierra Club Presidio Task Force and the Park Service each military foursome will be issued one of these.
1-14-94
The $3 million Gatling Golf Caddy when lowered into its firing position will fire 100 golf balls per minute.
©Phil (CAPTAIN HOOK) Frank

One of these new 'Smart Balls' can knock out a bird watcher at 200 yards!
However, the Gatling has a nasty left slice so compensate accordingly.

OPERATION DIVOT STORM NEARS ITS KICK-OFF TIME:

All of the 11 military foursomes will assemble here at the Presidio Golf Course clubhouse at 0730 tomorrow.

Each foursome will be equipped with Gatling Golf Caddies, 1,000 balls and M-16s disguised as golf clubs. These will fire rubber bullets.
At 0800 two foursomes will seize and hold the clubhouse...
1-15-94

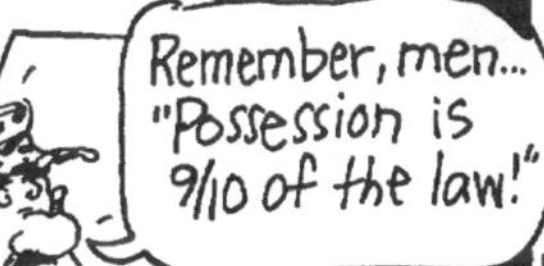
..while the other nine foursomes will deploy in each of the sand traps and secure the perimeter of the course from all Sierra Club Task Force members and Park Rangers.
Remember, men... "Possession is 9/10 of the law!"

Sir! May I ask why you've chosen an 0800 time for Operation Divot Storm?
It was the only tee-off time I could get!
Phil (I'LL BE IN THE BUNKER) Frank

...just another speed bump at the exit marked "Visitor Information"... fixing my flat tire in the "emergency parking only" lane of the high-tech highway...

© Phil (CAST YOUR FLAT TO THE WINDS.) Frank

I'm riding with you in the fast lane, Al!! You're in the driver's seat and we've got a load of technology on board!

The Orwell Diaries. Our feral cat's presence is requested at the Clinton White House, supposedly to stem a rodent invasion. Then he learns the ugly truth.

This morning I picked the lock on my door and got into the hallway of the White House basement. I was almost able to blow the lid off Whitewater...

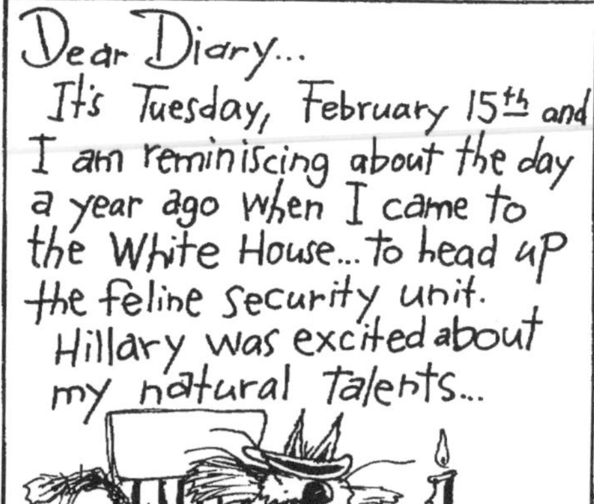
Dear Diary...
It's Tuesday, February 15th and I am reminiscing about the day a year ago when I came to the White House... to head up the feline security unit.
Hillary was excited about my natural talents...

THAT IDIOT CAT HAS SHREDDED THE CURTAINS IN THE ROSE ROOM!!
2-15-94

Now she has put me to work doing what I do best, but instead of curtains she has me shredding financial records.
SCREEE

Had Edwin Meese only known of my talents when he was Attorney-General, I could've gotten into politics years ago!!
Love,
Orwell
© Phil (CLAWS AND AFFECT) Frank

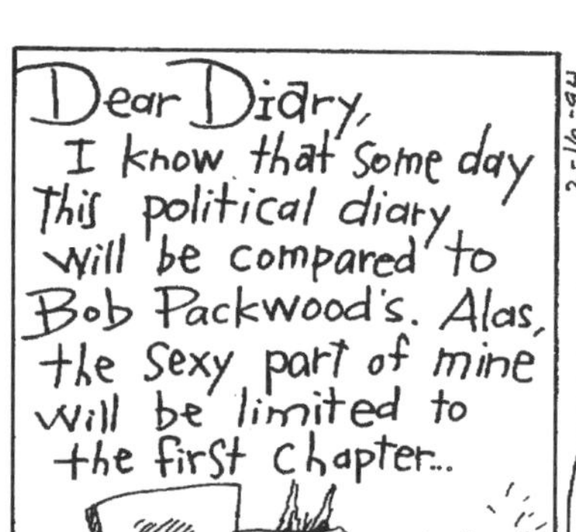
Dear Diary,
I know that some day this political diary will be compared to Bob Packwood's. Alas, the sexy part of mine will be limited to the first chapter...
2-16-94

... prior to my neutering to help out Bill's campaign to win the support of the bird lovers.
WE MUST CONTROL THE FERAL CAT POPULATION!
CLAP CLAP CLAP

I remember it clearly. Bill called me into the Oval Office. His words still ring in my ears:
Who here wants to keep his job?
ME-OW!
FELINE SECURITY
© Phil (PARTING IS SUCH "TWEET" SORROW) Frank
I was the first cat to sign up for the "JUST SAY YO TO DRUGS" campaign.
Anesthesia?
YO!!

Dear Diary,
Besides my job practicing my line ("I did it, your honor.") for the upcoming Whitewater investigation, I am also doing some late night chauffering.

That's one Super Cheeseburger, a large fries...
BURG HEAV
2-23-94

And two chocolate milk shakes. Will there be anything else, sir?
BZZZP
© Phil (HAIL TO THE CHEF.) Frank

How would you like to meet the President of the United States?
Nice try, hairball!

ALPHONSE, HAVING BEEN AWAKENED FROM HIBERNATION BY A BAD DREAM AND UNABLE TO GO BACK TO SLEEP, DIGS HIS WAY OUT OF THE BEARS' DEN:
SNIFF! SNIFF!
3-11-94

AS HIS EYES ADJUST TO THE BRIGHT GLARE OF THE SUN, HE IS APPROACHED BY TWO YOUTHS:
YO! CHECK OUT THE T-SHIRT!
GIANTS

GET WITH IT, DUDE! THE GIANTS GOT A NEW LOOK!
WHERE YOU BEEN?
GIANTS
©Phil NO SNIPE EFFECTS) Frank

Isn't that just like San Francisco? Lie down to take a little rest. Wake up and you're out of style.
GIANTS

ALPHONSE, THE FIRST BEAR TO LEAVE THE HIBERNATION DEN, IS SLOW TO PICK UP ON RECENT NEWS ITEMS:
The President... Whitewater. Hmmm... He must be going rafting.
DRUGS
GIANTS

Excuse me, ma'am. Who is Tonya Harding?
WHO'S TONYA HARDING? YOU BEEN ASLEEP FOR FOUR MONTHS??
3-17-94

WELL, AS A MATTER OF FACT I HAVE BEEN! SO THERE!
GIANTS
©Phil THE GOOD, THE BAD AND THE SNUGGLY) Frank

THREE STRIKES... YOU'RE OUT!! THREE STRIKES... YOU'RE OUT!!
Baseball! At least that I understand!
LOCK 'EM UP!
THROW AWAY THE KEYS!
GIANTS

Excuse me, sir... you look like a man of intelligence. I can tell by the way you wear your baseball cap backwards!
GIANTS

I'd like to introduce you to a new product specially designed for a person of your mentality!!
Baseball caps that are manufactured backwards!!
GIANTS
4-24-93

Admittedly they cost more, but look at what you get... A quick-release adjustable strap in the front and the bill is attached in the back!!
©Phil THE BILL'S IN THE MAIL) Frank

What'll they think of next?

STILL ADJUSTING TO LIFE ABOVE GROUND AFTER FOUR MONTHS IN THE HIBERNATION DEN, ALPHONSE PICKS UP A CHRONICLE SPORTS SECTION:
Let's see how Will Clark is doing in Scottsdale... Hee.. hee...

HUH?
WHERE'S WILL?
HE'S NOT EVEN ON THE ROSTER!!
3-22-94

WHAT HAVE YOU DONE WITH WILL CLARK?
I didn't do anything with him, man! His contract expired. He went to the Texas Rangers!
©Phil Frank (FOR BATTER OR WORSE)

Got a 5150... Corner of Sutter and Market. Bear having a breakdown.
Sob.. The Texas Rangers..

THE MAYOR CONSULTS HIS MAGIC MIRROR:
Mayor, Mayor on the wall... who's the fairest leader of them all?

You are, oh mighty one. You alone..
Frank!! You're not dyeing your hair anymore! So, it's true! Looks much better!!
4-19-94

Shhh! 'Tis our secret! Yours and mine alone!!
If that be so, master then why didst I read it in Herb Caen?
©Phil Frank (IT'S ALL DONE WITH MIRRORS.)

How do you get newspapers delivered in there?
Mister mayor, the Careers Day student is...
WHOOPS! We'll come back later!

Hilda's Home Safety Hints..
4-23-94

Homeowners should be aware of a common household danger that occurs each year during fishing season.
You know what I'm referring to...

Allowing oil-soaked smoked salmon to build up in kitchens, hallways and stairwells can only lead to one thing...

CHOMP!!
©Phil Frank (WHERE THERE'S SMOKE THERE'S SALMON)
Spontaneous consumption. Don't let it happen to you!
urp!
GIA

ALPHONSE GETS THE BAD NEWS IN THE CHRON:
CITY DUMPSTER
OH NO!!

4-25-94
THIS CAN'T BE!! NOT NOW! THE GIANTS NEED HIM!!
What's wrong, Alphonse?

Look at this headline, Hilda: "BONDS HITTING ALL TIME LOW!" The Giants need Barry's bat!!
Let me see that...
©Phil Frank (ALL THE NEWS THAT FLITS)
ER
You nut! That's the business section!!
Oh.

AT THE SAN FRANCISCO MINT:
We've received the resume of an individual who may be able to deal with our mouse problem. He has served as Chief of Feline Security at the White House.
Let's offer him a job!

3-24-94
IN ORWELL'S WHITE HOUSE DETENTION ROOM:
Letter for you from San Francisco!

I'M HIRED!! NOW I JUST HAVE TO GET OUT OF HERE!!

ESCAPE PLAN, PHASE II: "SOCKS" DISGUISE.
©Phil Frank (CAST YOUR FACE TO THE WIND)

Ted Danson... eat your heart out!

ORWELL'S BEEN HIRED BY THE SAN FRANCISCO MINT TO RID IT OF MICE, BUT HE MUST FIRST ESCAPE HIS WHITE HOUSE INCARCERATION:
WHITE-WATER WITNESS DETENTION

TO DO THIS HE IS EMPLOYING HIS "SOCKS" DISGUISE:
Now I just have to get outside...
3-25-94

SOCKS!! What happened to you? You look awful! You must've had a rough night. Want to go out?
MEOOOOWR!
©Phil Frank (A GOING-AWAY GIFT)

YUCK!! CHELSEA! ISN'T SOCKS HOUSEBROKEN?
TAXI!

The S.S. Jeremiah O'Brien, last operational ship of the fleet of Liberty ships that took part in the D-Day invasion fifty years prior, was departing San Francisco for the ceremonies celebrating the anniversary of the Normandy landing. I was jealous of Carl Nolte, ace Chronicle reporter who got to go on the trip and send in daily dispatches to the paper. The best **I** could do was send one of my characters.

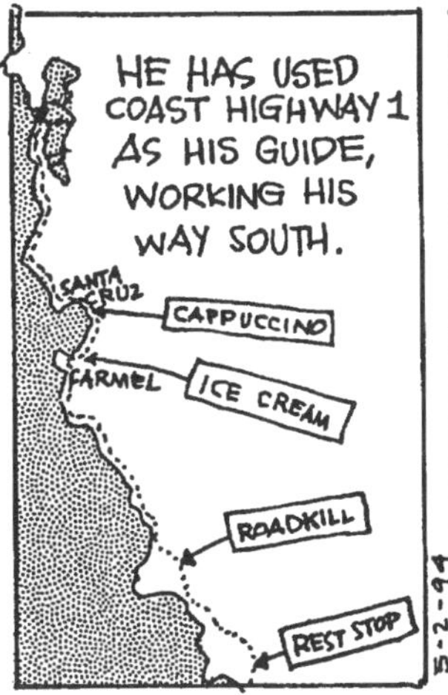

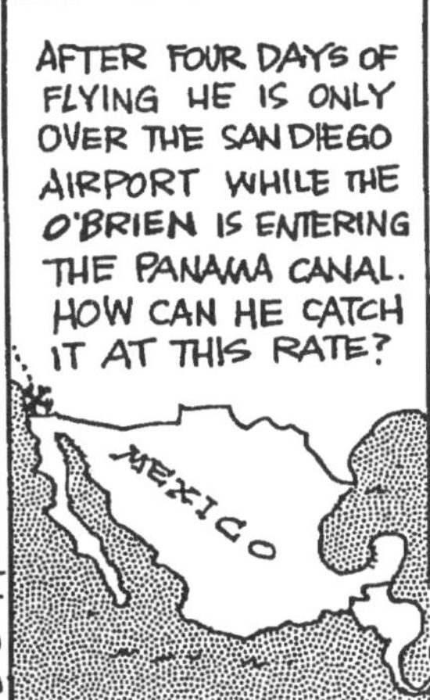

"The steady throb of the engine resonates even up here in the crow's nest, from whence I survey the ship and the sea...

5-18-94

"The crew is downright friendly, treating me more like one of the family than as a stowaway. Having the only cask of brandy aboard has served me well for purposes of barter. Spirits are high!"

THE JEREMIAH O'BRIEN PLOWS EASTWARD TOWARD EUROPE. PLEASANT DAYS PROVIDE AMPLE TIME FOR READING:

THE SHIP'S LIBRARY HAS BEEN EMPTIED OF ALL THE GREAT CLASSICS THAT MAKE PERFECT READING FOR AN OCEAN VOYAGE:
"Caine Mutiny"
"Moby Dick"
"Distant Islands"
5-21-94

"The Cruel Sea" by Monsarrat...
"Lieutenant Hornblower" by C.S. Forester...
© Phil (ONLY TWO PIECES OF CARRION) Frank
Man... this is the life.
FLATTENED FAUNA
A FIELD GUIDE TO ROADKILL

Fax from Bruce in England!
Thanks.
5-23-94

"Dear Farley,
We made it to the Portsmouth Navy Yard in England. We received an amazing greeting upon arrival...

"I think every sea gull in the British Isles came out to welcome the O'Brien and freeload food scraps...
© Phil (I GUANO GO HOME NOW) Frank

"I felt like James Brown at an Elvis impersonators' convention."

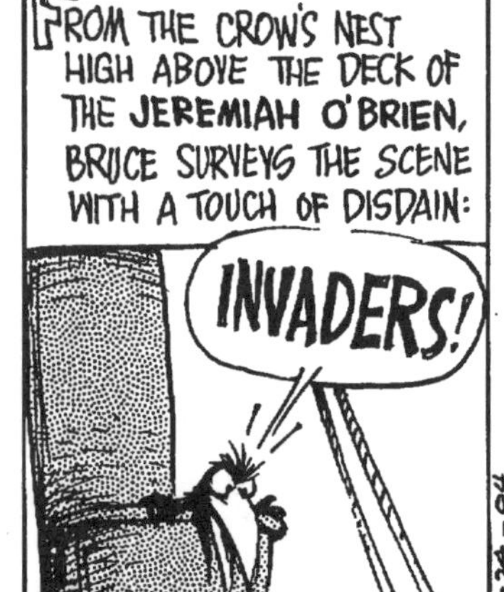

FROM THE CROW'S NEST HIGH ABOVE THE DECK OF THE JEREMIAH O'BRIEN, BRUCE SURVEYS THE SCENE WITH A TOUCH OF DISDAIN:
INVADERS!

THE SHIP HAS BEEN OPENED TO VISITORS IN THE NAVY YARD AT PORTSMOUTH IN SOUTHERN ENGLAND:
RAKE THE DECKS!! ANGLO-SAXON HORDES ON THE GUNNELS!!
5-24-94

TEA DRINKERS IN THE SCUPPERS!! ROYALISTS WITH INSTAMATICS ON THE AFTERDECK!! GIVE ME A LIBERTY SHIP OR GIVE ME DEATH!
© Phil (ONE IF BY LAND, TWO IF BY TOUR BOAT) Frank
"WHERE CAN A GUY GET A DRINK AROUND HERE?!
The Yanks haven't changed much in 50 years.
CLICK!

WHILE VISITORS TOUR THE JEREMIAH O'BRIEN IN ENGLAND, BRUCE HIDES OUT IN THE SHIP'S CROW'S NEST AND WRITES IN HIS DIARY:
5-31-94
Dear Diary,
Being back in the land of my ancestors causes me to recall those days of long ago when, as a fledgling, I sat on grandfather's lap.

Aye.. I'll tell ye, lad, the war years were rough ones, they were... rationing... blackouts... buzzbombs... fears of a German invasion..
What did YOU do in the war, grandpap?
© Phil THE CAW OF THE WILD Frank

I was one of the queen's ravens in the Tower of London, lad. People were all talking about the Allies invading France...
I'd always heard about these French ravens, so...
This is the part I like best...

BRUCE CONTINUES TO REMINISCE ABOUT HIS GRANDFATHER NIGEL'S WAR STORIES:
So there oi am in the Tower of London, one of the queen's own ravens, Brucie, me boy.
YEAH?!
6-1-94

We all knew the invasion of France was coming soon but we needed to link up with the French Underground. So I volunteered to go.
Really?

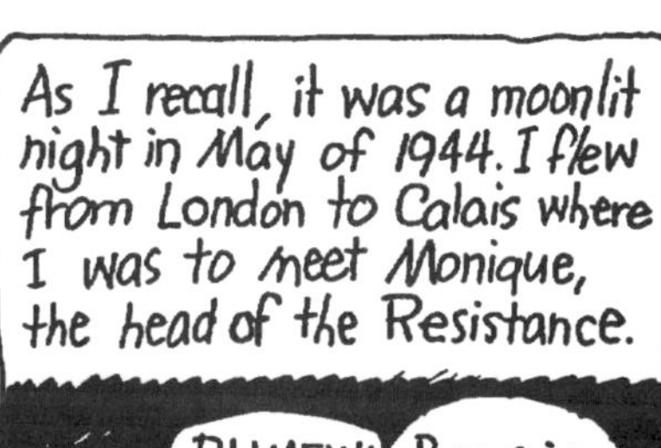
As I recall, it was a moonlit night in May of 1944. I flew from London to Calais where I was to meet Monique, the head of the Resistance.

BLIMEY!!
Bon soir, monsieur.
© Phil TOUJOUR GAI Frank

As I recall there wasn't all that much resistance on her part.
GRANDMA!

AS THE FLOTILLA OF SHIPS NEARS THE NORMANDY COAST TO HONOR THIS, THE 50TH ANNIVERSARY OF D-DAY, A RAVEN LIFTS OFF FROM THE S.S. JEREMIAH O'BRIEN:
6-6-94

UP... UP HE CLIMBS INTO THE MORNING SKY UNTIL THE BEACHES AND THE CEREMONIES AND THE GATHERED THRONGS ARE BUT DISTANT IMAGES...

AND THEN HE ROLLS SLOWLY AND DROPS IN A DIZZYING SPIRAL OF SWEEPS AND LOOPS IN AN AERIAL SALUTE TO THE MANY WHO FOUGHT AND FELL THERE 50 YEARS AGO TODAY...
© Phil THANK YOU. Frank

CAUSING AN OFFICIAL TO EXCLAIM: "THIS WAS NOT ON THE PROGRAM."
It was on mine.

ORWELL IS STUDYING SOME OF THE LOCAL BIRD LIFE IN GOLDEN GATE PARK:
Looks like a little territorial squabble in progress...
5-19-94

Why... it's a female Canvas-backed Bird Wooer and a male Large-bellied Feline Feeder...

You're feeding those disgusting feral cats and they're decimating the songbirds!!
Stuff it, bird brain!

Don't think we'll be seeing any mating dances today.
© Phil (PUT YOUR LEFT FIST IN... TAKE YOUR...) Frank

THE FERAL CATS OF GOLDEN GATE PARK MEET FOR THEIR WEEKLY THERAPY SESSION:
My name is Roscoe and I'm a recovering birdoholic.
We're here for you, Roscoe!

I wish to share with you a recent temptation I spurned on Telegraph Hill...
Let's hear it, Roscoe!
Tell us, brother!
5-20-94

I was coming up the Filbert Steps when I heard an awful racket. There, not two feet above, were a dozen wild parrots, intoxicated on fermented berries, in a Pyracantha bush!
What stopped you, friend?
© Phil (CAT-OF-EIGHT-TAILS) Frank

My belief that I could control my passions stopped me!
AMEN, BROTHER!
And a lady who swung a mop like a nine iron.

THE CHANNEL ONE ONE-EYE NEWS TEAM'S MORNING REPORT:
Well, Connie, it looks like the Florida Citrus folks aren't too happy with their newest spokesman.
Right you are, Dick.

Stagnant sales and a national boycott are causing the Citrus Commission to consider a less controversial spokesman than Rush Limbaugh.

Howard Nichols reports...

Connie.. I'm here at Golden Gate Park where, in spite of heated denials, what appear to be test commercials with a different spokesman are being shot.
© Phil (GOPHER BROKE) Frank 6-24-94

I'm feral, I'm neutered and I love orange juice with my breakfast!
?

YES! WE HAVE THE NEW Wonderbra

The hype surrounding the arrival of the **Wonderbra** in San Francisco was astounding. Brinks trucks bringing in the shipment of brassieres... women waiting in lines a block long to get into the stores. Something had to be done to lampoon this cleavage quest, so why not have Bruin Hilda get one? The problem for me was figuring out how many cups a bear's brassiere would have. I called the bear specialist at Yosemite. Her answer? Six cups.

Dear Members of the U.N. Population Conference...

It is with great interest that we sterilized felines read about your human population problems...

The way things are going, with 90 million births a year, you are going to be up to your fanny packs in babies pretty soon.!!

9-12-94

We neutered cats and dogs wish to offer our help in the same way you humans have helped us curb our population.

© Phil (SUTURE SELF) Frank

Hey, Baba... what did you call me about?
I'm working on a medical break-through for California
Let's see... one ounce of sunblock...
9-27-94

My secret formula contains...
"Patch of Spandex,
Italian shoe,
Part from B. M. W. ...
Free-range chicken,
hormone free
Scab from roller-blader's knee."

Mix it thoroughly and take two tablespoons daily. It tastes awful!
What'll it do for me?
WHRRR
©Phil (YOUR MONEY OR YOUR LIFESTYLE) Frank
It'll extend your lifestyle expectancy up to four years.
Hmm... Needs a little arugula.

THE TWO AFRICAN GOLIATH FROGS, JUST ARRIVED FROM ANGELS CAMP, LUNCH AT THE FOG CITY:
WAITER!!
10-12-94

Look at my soup! What do you see in it?
um... a fly..

A FLY! YES.. A FLY! ONE LOUSY FLY! YOU SHOULD BE ASHAMED TO PUT FLY SOUP ON YOUR MENU!
I'll be right back.
©Phil (CAPTAIN CUISINE) Frank

I saw one go through here a minute ago..
They're never around when you want them..

THE METROPOLITAN TRANSPORTATION COMMITTEE HOLDS A MEETING TO GET PUBLIC INPUT ON TRAFFIC SOLUTIONS:
State your name, please.
Ted Braneless.
10-14-94

Again and again I have heard people call for concrete solutions to Bay Area traffic congestion.
Here's a concrete solution: MORE HIGHWAYS!!

We're looking for alternatives to more highways and driving..
Alternatives? What alternative is there to driving?
©Phil (Insufficient Dada) Frank

Your feet?
MY FEET? YO' MAMA!!

The Maltese Falcon was going on the auction block at Christie's. A contingent of San Franciscans was headed for New York to take part in the bidding, hoping to acquire it and put it on display in **John's Grill** - Dashiell Hammett's old hangout.

I was waiting at the **Chronicle** for a phoned-in result of the bidding so I could put it in the next day's cartoon. We thought it would go for about $80,000. Final price was $398,500. YIKES!!

IT'S A COLD MONDAY IN THE **BIG APPLE**. I'M IN NEW YORK CITY. SAM SPADE ASKED ME TO PULL OFF THE NEAR IMPOSSIBLE:

HE TOLD ME TO BRING THE BIRD BACK TO SAN FRANCISCO. I'M TALKING FALCON... THE "MALTESE FALCON"
12-5-94

I SLIP INTO **CHRISTIE'S** SHOWROOM ON 67TH STREET, AND THERE IT IS... JUST LIKE SAM SAID IT WOULD BE... FIFTY-FIVE POUNDS OF LEAD WITH A BRONZE PATINA..
What a bird!

© Phil (THE MALTESE PIGEON) Frank

TOMORROW THE BIRD GOES ON THE BLOCK... THE OPENING BID WILL BE 30 G'S. I'VE GOT A WAD IN MY POCKET. I'LL BE THE "BEARD"... THE MYSTERY BIDDER FOR **JOHN'S GRILL** BACK IN SAN FRANCISCO:

I just hope I don't stand out in the crowd.
76

IT'S BIDDING TIME AT CHRISTIE'S IN NEW YORK:
I'm getting nervous... we're three lots away from the Maltese Falcon...
12-6-94

Everything's in place. I see John Konstin from John's Grill. I'm the "beard" for John. I'll do the bidding for him on the statue...

There's Lee Houskeeper with his cellular phone hook-up to San Francisco. He's scanning the crowd for me.
THE BID ON THE TASMANIAN DEATH MASK STANDS AT $1800. DO I HEAR $2,000?
© Phil (FOR BIDDER OR WORSE) Frank

Psst, Lee!!
TWO THOUSAND TO THE SHORT GUY IN THE BACK ROW!
Uh-oh.

CHRISTIE'S AUCTION HOUSE IN NEW YORK IS EMPTY EXCEPT FOR ONE DISAPPOINTED BIDDER IN THE BACK ROW:
I can't believe it...

The Maltese Falcon sold for $398,500. I was never even in the running!
12-7-94

I'll be going back to San Francisco empty-handed... except, of course, for my unintentional bid when I waved at a friend..
Your package, Sir.
© Phil (A BIDDER PILL TO SWALLOW) Frank
A Tasmanian death mask for $2000. Jeeesh!!

TREES
You really like this tree, Olive?
Sort of.

It's kind of lopsided— most of the branches are on one side of it. The trunk is twisted.
Uh huh...
12-20-94

And look... it's already losing its needles.
True.
©Phil (VISIT OUR BRANCH OFFICE) Frank

Sir. We in the evergreen industry prefer to think of such a tree as being botanically challenged.
We'll take it.

Fare thee well, good friend. What leonine plumage graces my avian cohort this gilded dayspring!!

And what a fulvous, honey-paled dawning it is that peeks through the gossamer fog that hangs on Berkeley's highlands.
12-26-94

As counterpoint, our coniferous sapling hangs its limp limbs as the very symbol of a waning holiday.
©Phil (WORDS TO LISP BY) Frank

And lo!...my laundry... see how it lies in languid disarray.
I'd like to strangle whoever gave him a thesaurus for Christmas.

Here's your new calendar, Farley.
Thanks, Eric.
12-30-94

1995 already.... 1995...there's something about that year... What is it?
OH, NO!

It'll have been twenty years in 1995 that I've been doing this... TWENTY YEARS!!
I've got to get some air!!

My every experience... my very existence is dictated by the whims of another.
BEEP!!
©Phil (IT'S SO BLACK AND WHITE) Frank
The truth is painfully clear...
I'm ink... therefore I am.

Cartoonists as an endangered species? 1995 was to be the year of the Dwindling Number of Greats. On the first day of January Gary Larson's "Far Side" disappeared from the daily papers. Within a month Berke Breathed announced the demise of "Outland," his "Bloom County" spin-off, and by the end of the year Bill Watterson's "Calvin and Hobbes" was gone. Was it global warming or a meteorite that caused the great comic die-off? Got me.

Baba... what's wrong?
I haven't the slightest idea.
1-24-95

I was answering my e-mail and then I switched over to the Alternative Sex conference on the Internet. My computer started to overheat... went **POOF** and the screen went black.
Hmm...

Excuse me. Are you a Mister ReBok, first name Baba?
That's me and this is the machine.
©Phil (A BIG BYTE OUT OF YOUR POCKETBOOK) Frank
This is the part of the Information Superhighway that nobody tells you about...

So... what's got you so distressed this time, Farley?
Something's missing in my life and there's no way to replace it.
1-26-95

Gary Larson's weird, occasionally sick sense of humor is gone. I'm having trouble coping without that perspective on the world since he retired.
I see...
The only other cartoon that keeps me going is the politically incorrect humor of Berkeley Breathed's **Outland** on Sundays. Thank heavens that...
He's retiring March 26th.
©Phil (ALL THE NEWS THAT CAUSES FITS) Frank

Maybe I should've been a bit gentler with that news item.

IRENE FINDS A ROSE AND A CARD ON HER SCOOTER:
"Valentine greetings to the maid I admire,
From the guy in your life with the chalk on his tire.

I find that I wander in an emotional thicket,
For the only love notes you write
Arrive on a ticket
2-14-95

When on deadline I find that I stare at the clock,
Aware, as I write, that you're circling the block.
©Phil (TERMS OF ENTRAPMENT) Frank
When I see your tender missive on my windshield tomorrow,
I'll know again that for me... Parking is such sweet sorrow."

The year 1995 was the Chinese Year of the Pig and, coincidentally, a lot of attention was being paid to the Bay Area's feral pig population. Part of this gang of porcine roto-rooters was tearing up the watershed land, especially the hillsides of Mount Tamalpais in Marin County.

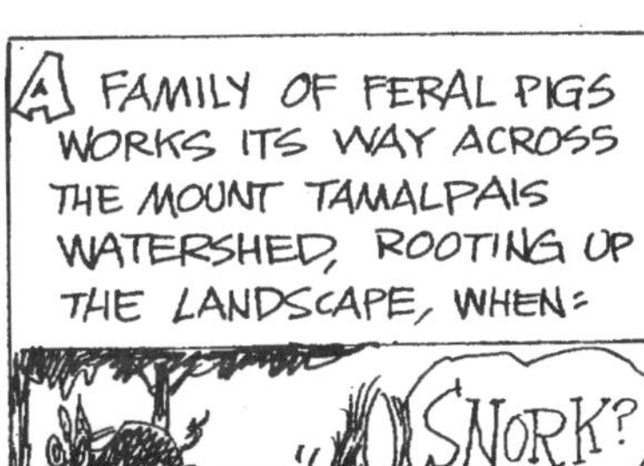

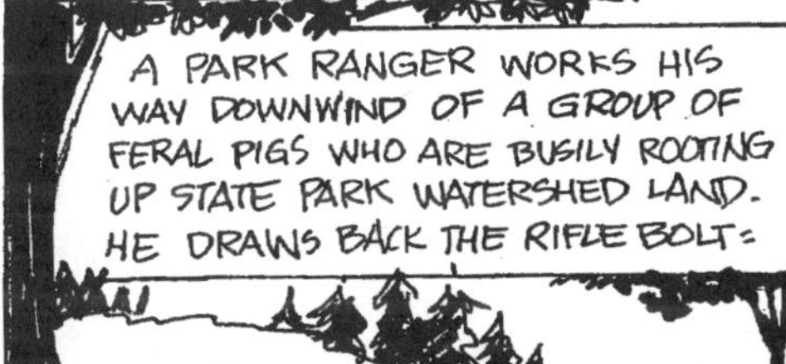

WHOA!! DON'T SHOOT!! CHINESE YEAR OF THE PIG! WILD BOAR ARE EXEMPTED BY THE DEPARTMENT OF THE INTERIOR UNTIL FEBRUARY 1996! RULES & REGULATIONS HANDBOOK... PAGE 362!!

2-8-95

Neon lights glistened off Ellis Street in the foggy night...
EAT
The Maltese Falcon was coming to San Francisco, specifically John's Grill, Hammett's old hangout.
The story lent itself to a cartoon noir treatment - with Bruce the Raven as the private eye hired to protect the Falcon. The series was a break from my usual style. I had a lot of fun with these strips.

THE CITY BAKED UNDER A BRIGHT SUN WHILE I WAITED FOR A CALL THAT MIGHT NEVER COME.
Mister Raven!!
4-3-95
You know how you've been waiting anxiously for some word from a Mister Spade about the Maltese Falcon?
Is he here, Babs?
No... but a gentleman by the name of Farley would like to see you.
Oh. Send him in.
© Phil (A REMARKABLE DEDUCTION) Frank
Mister Raven will see you now.
First of all... I want you to know I have nothing against the concept of an office in the home, Bruce... but...

PERHAPS MY PATIENCE HAD FINALLY PAID OFF. THIS COULD BE THE CALL I'D BEEN WAITING FOR.
RING!
4-4-95
I'm looking for a private eye named Raven. That you? Good. This is Spade. Sam Spade.
I'm sending a little job your way, kid. There's a certain bird headed for Frisco soon. Ever heard of the Falcon?.. the Maltese Falcon? Yeah... I thought so
© Phil (THE LONG WING OF THE LAW) Frank
The Falcon's going to need some protection. You available?
I always get my bird, Sam.

Sam Spade... Sam Spade actually called me... he wants me to guard the Maltese Falcon...

4-5-95
It'll be at John's Grill in late April. Someone might try to heist the dingus. After all... it's worth 400 G's...

I'd better case Hammett's hideout now so there'll be no surprises
I'll be back later, Babs.
YES, MISTER RAVEN.
© Phil Frank MY BIO IS DEGRADABLE

Oh, Bruce... when you're leaving would you put out the recycling?
Get a life, Pal!

A TOOTHLESS GRIN OF A MOON HUNG OVER ELLIS STREET AS I CASED THE SCENE OUTSIDE JOHN'S GRILL:
4-12-95
John's Grill
STEAKS & SEAFOOD
COCKTAILS
63

DASHIELL HAMMETT HUNG HIS HAT HERE WHILE HE PENNED "THE MALTESE FALCON" AND IT WAS HERE THE REAL BIRD WOULD SOON APPEAR. NOW THE STATUE'S WORTH A COOL 400 GS...

Sam Spade wants me to be in charge of security.

I could use a drink.

The usual, Luis.
Sure thing, Mister Raven.
© Phil Frank HERE'S MUD IN YOUR EAR

"Mister Raven"... I could get used to that.
One Roadkill... on the rocks.

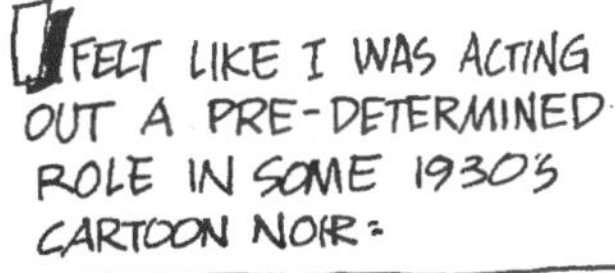
I FELT LIKE I WAS ACTING OUT A PRE-DETERMINED ROLE IN SOME 1930'S CARTOON NOIR:

Neon lights glistened off Ellis Street in the foggy night...

HERE I WAS WORKING SECURITY FOR BOGART'S "MALTESE FALCON" AT JOHN'S GRILL, DASHIELL HAMMETT'S HANGOUT:
I spotted the local gumshoe. He owed me a favor.

4-13-95
Someone's going to try to cop the statue of the bird... I'm sure of it. I need your help!
Round up ze usual suspects.
Oui, mon capitan.
© Phil Frank PLAY THAT 'TOON

Nice try, millet breath. Wrong script. This is "The Maltese Falcon" not "Casablanca".
We'll always have Paris.

I STUDIED THE SHIFTING SHADOWS OF THE CITY AT NIGHT. A POTHOLED, RUTTED ELLIS STREET MIRRORED THE ROAD MY OWN LIFE HAD TAKEN:
Sigh.
4-19-95

A private eye with a 98¢ bag of millet seed to my name and my office rent due... and here I am putting my life on the line to protect a bird that's worth close to half a mil...
MALTESE FALCON HERE APRIL 28

Two birds take two different flight paths... one ends up worth 400 Gs and the other... a two-bit P.I. whose guardian angel got a better offer.
© Phil (GET THE LEAD OUT) Frank

Of course, the bird who ended up worth $400,000 also ended up with 52 pounds of lead in him.
What a way to go.

It just doesn't seem proper for the pontiff to get into this sort of thing, Orwell.
Oh?
4-18-95

First of all... I believe in the separation of church and state! Secondly I believe in the separation of church and professional sports!!
What are you talking about, Speedbump?

THIS HEADLINE!!
49ers get a jump on draft by signing Pope
You ninny!! That's Marquez Pope, a Rams free agent!!
© Phil (TAIL OF TWO PSYCHES) Frank
Oh.
A mind is a terrible thing.

Good morning. I'm with Megatrends polls.
FOG CITY
What political party are you registered with?
Vegetarian.

Okay... Do you intend to vote in the November election?
Yes!
And which candidate are you voting for?
Woodrow Wilson.
5-1-95

And what is his political affiliation?
Deceased.
I see. What is your racial background?
Beaver.
And... How old are you.
Six.
© Phil (CD ROM DAS) Frank
Thank you for your time.
That ought to throw a kink in the computer.

Panhandling was getting more and more aggressive in San Francisco. The public was getting frustrated and put off by the incessant pressure.

Seemed like an occasion for a touch of sensibility, so Beppo stepped in to give his cronies a lesson or two in urban manners.

Hmm...

A Chronicle reader wrote a letter to the editor complaining about the long-windedness of certain letter writers and suggested that authors be limited to **haiku** to present their opinions. I thought it a good idea, too. Baba's fax was inundated and for awhile there was a flurry of them printed in the paper.

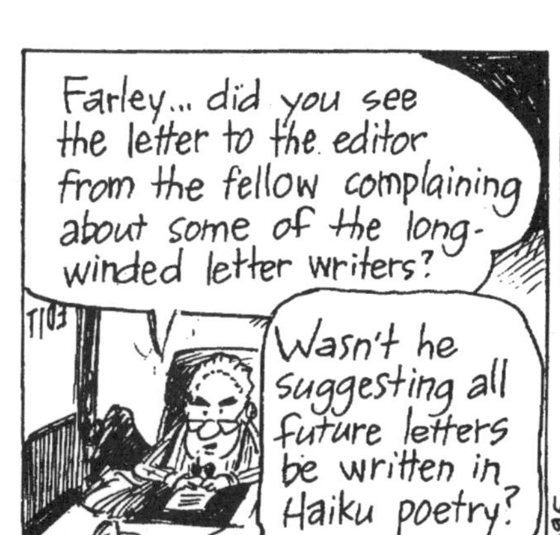
Farley... did you see the letter to the editor from the fellow complaining about some of the long-winded letter writers?
Wasn't he suggesting all future letters be written in Haiku poetry?

EXACTLY!! I think he's on to something! I'm going to try it: From now on... all letters to the editor must be in Haiku...
Three lines of seventeen syllables...
5-24-95

five syllables in the first line... seven in the second... five in the third.
EDITOR
Can you do it?
© Phil (TREE VERSE) Frank
"Rainforest laid low. 'Wake up and smell the ozone' Says man with chainsaw."
Very good!!

IN AN EFFORT TO CURTAIL LONG-WINDED LETTER WRITERS, THE DAILY REQUIREMENT NOW DEMANDS THAT ALL WRITERS MAKE THEIR POINTS IN HAIKU, JAPANESE POEMS COMPOSED OF 17 SYLLABLES:
HAIKU?

Let's see... five syllables, first line... seven in the second five in the third...
5-25-95

"Jack-booted Fed agents..." Darn! That's six syllables.. "Jack-booted Fed cops..." Good! Second line... "Breaking down my front door..."
One...two... three... four... five... six...
© Phil (THE RHYMES THAT TRY MENS' SOULS) Frank
Drat!! That's only six syllables...
This is tough!

THE DAILY REQUIREMENT'S LETTERS TO THE EDITOR HAVE BECOME REQUIRED READING NOW THAT AUTHORS MUST WRITE THEM IN HAIKU:
"Willie (Speaker) Brown. Will he speak softer now that His term is recalled."
How about this one? "G. Gordon Liddy. His mouth opens. Chill breeze blows. Please shut the window."
"Luxury models. One hundred per cent tariffs. My Nissan worth more."
"Clinton's feet of sand Should mix water and cement. And then they will stand."
"All those nuts with guns Should be rounded up and shot. What am I saying?"
Phil (FEED THE METRE) Frank
5-26-95

A subdued group of costumed animals makes its way through the sand dunes to Ocean Beach for a memorial service:

AHEM! We are gathered here today, fur-bearing creatures one and all, to remember a rare individual among the human species... a man who, through humor, music and whimsy was able to teach folks to laugh at adversity and at themselves.
He could even make a ground hog in an Elvis get-up giggle. I know. I'm that ground hog!
© Phil (EVERY CLOUD SHOULD HAVE A SILVER LINING) Frank
Steve Silver, creator of Beach Blanket Babylon, proved to all of us an important axiom: "Silliness is next to godliness!"
We'll miss you, Steve.
Bye, Steve.
Bye.

SIGN UP
A plethora of candidates were entering the mayoral race so it seemed like a good idea to toss a bear into the pot. Bruin Hilda's slogan became "Hilda... Fur a Change." The Chronicle got into the act, producing a red, white and blue placard for the news racks reading HILDA FOR MAYOR. They ran an extra 5,000 copies as posters. It was fun to see them in people's windows.

I worry when you get that look in your eyes, Hilda...
I'm thinking... I'm just thinking...
Not a single one of these declared mayoral candidates represents the interests of the animals of San Francisco!!
FOG CITY V DUMPSTER
PATIO DINING
Minorities are represented... Gays are too... so are conservatives and liberals but not animals!
If I ran for mayor I could have every last animal vote!!
© Phil (DON'T PARADE ON MY REIGN) Frank
But, Hilda... animals don't vote!
Must you be such a pragmatist!

HILDA AND HER POLITICAL ADVISOR SIT ON THE DUMPSTER'S PATIO AND DISCUSS THE MAYORAL ELECTION:
Don't do it, Hilda!
I could be the dark horse.

While Jordan and company are sniping at each other I would play the role of reason and sensibility!

They'd all wake up one morning and they'd find a bear in charge of the city!
©Phil (DOES A BEAR SIT IN THE PATIO?) Frank
Yeah... It'd be a regular Pooh d'etat!
Does Clint Reilly get paid if his client loses?

As your "Interim Campaign Chairman Against My Better Judgment" I'd like to review some upcoming events.
Shoot.
GIANTS

Thursday, June 14th... Meet with Possum Anti-Defamation League at 4 p.m. ... Urban Pet Coalition at 5 p.m... Friday the 16th... Black and White Ball...
6-6-95

Saturday... kick-off press conference at Moose's at 1 p.m.! Sunday... March in the Gay Freedom Day Parade. Any questions?
©Phil (CLAWS CELEBRE) Frank
What should I wear to the Black and White Ball?...
Well... at least we've got our priorities straight!

THE MIDNIGHT OIL BURNS AFTER HOURS AT THE CAMPAIGN HEADQUARTERS OF HILDA FOR MAYOR:
We need a really pithy campaign slogan!!
Describe pithy.

Like "Hilda... She Cares" or... "Vote For Change... Vote Bruin Hilda".
How about "HILDA... FUR A CHANGE"
Hmm...
6-7-95

"WHEN YOU CARE ENOUGH TO ELECT THE VERY BEAST!"
"CROSS THE JORDAN... VOTE FOR HILDA!"
WAIT!! I'VE GOT IT!
©Phil (THIS BEARS WATCHING) Frank
"Tired of the others? Try a new species!"
Nice try, Floyd.

The media will be seated here. At exactly 10 a.m. I will introduce you as the next mayor of San Francisco and you will approach the podium, Hilda. Okay... go!
HILDA FOR MAYOR

CUT! CUT! HOLD IT!!
?

Hilda... we've got a problem here. We can't run a naked candidate. Wear a dress for the press conference.
But.. I've got a coat of fur...
6-12-95

© Phil Frank (HAIR TODAY, GONE TOMORROW)
Which reminds me- The Anti-Fur League of Bernal Heights has pulled its endorsement!
WHAT'LL I DO?
You could always shave.

I'm sure you're aware of Robert Dole's recent assertion that Hollywood is lowering the nation's moral values.
Uh, yes...
HILDA FOR MAYOR
6-13-95

Isn't it true that you personally starred in a movie recently, Ms. Bear?
That would've been a romantic comedy I did in the mid '80s entitled "Never Cry Bear". It received a G rating.
HILDA

© Phil Frank (PUT IT ON!)
I was referring to "Strapless in Seattle"
NOW.. I CAN EXPLAIN THAT!!
Is there a spin doctor in the house?

Along the lines of the previous question... in relation to movies and morals, Ms. Bear....
Yes?
HILDA FOR MAYOR
6-14-95

It has been suggested that "The Bridges of Madison County" endorses and glorifies infidelity.
It does?
Do you plan to see it?
© Phil Frank (STAY WITH THE GROUP, PLEASE)

I can unequivocally state here and now, that I shall never see "The Bridges of Madison County"!
Thank you.
That was easy! She hates travelogues.
CLAP! CLAP!

HILDA'S PRESS CONFERENCE CONTINUES:
Ms. Bear... The public is well aware that you are an animal rights candidate and that you will seek to give fur-bearing mammals a voice in city government...
That's correct.
6-15-95
You are probably also aware that the primary victims of weapons are animals.
I am aware of that...
Where do you stand on the right to bear arms?
Speaking for myself, let me say...
HILDA
©Phil (I GAVE AT THE BUNKER) Frank
SUPPORT YOUR RIGHT TO ARM BEARS!!
Uh... every political viewpoint has its fringe element...
HILDA

THE TROOPS GATHER FOR COCKTAILS IN FARLEY'S SOMA LOFT PRIOR TO TONIGHT'S BLACK & WHITE BALL:
Last time I was in this building it was a fertilizer warehouse!
WHEW!
Irene... you are one great looking meter maid!
Careful. I have my violation book in my purse.
So... are you with security?
No. I'm with the Giants. They're playing in Seattle tonight.
Really... you don't think it's too much?
HILDA FOR MAYOR
The dress is definitely you, Hilda!
Baba... care for a little more transcendental medication?
6-16-95
©Phil (TRAV CHIC) Frank

AN AIR OF BARELY CONTAINED PANIC HAS SET IN AT THE BRUIN HILDA FOR MAYOR CAMPAIGN HEADQUARTERS
"STRAPLESS IN SEATTLE"?
6-20-95
YOU MAKE A MOVIE LIKE THAT AND DON'T TELL YOUR CAMPAIGN MANAGER?
It seemed so innocent at the time. He said it was a nature film.
GIANT
©Phil (DIGIT GOES TO HOLLYWOOD) Frank
AND YOU... SCREAMING OUT "SUPPORT YOUR RIGHT TO ARM BEARS" IN THE MIDDLE OF A PRESS CONFERENCE!!
Sorry.
WHAT ELSE?
GIANTS
The latest poll results are in. Who would've thought it was possible to slip below single digits.

Yes, madam?
I'd like to direct a question to the animal rights candidate, Bruin Hilda.

Why should I, a resident of the Sunset district, want to have a bear as mayor?
6-23-95

Well, I'm quick-witted. Bears are considered to have the highest intelligence of all mammals. We're noble beasts, honored by many cultures, worshipped as gods by some.
What **more** could you ask for in a mayor?

©Phil (FUR BE IT FROM ME!) Frank
She sounds like Willie Brown with fur.
Hmpf!

Hilda!! Check out this story I spotted in the Chron about Angela! Her political goose is cooked, baby!!
Oh?

"Angela Offers Rebel Leader Vice Presidency" I sent out a major press piece on this! You, my furry candidate, are one step closer to being mayor!
Let me see that!
HILDA FOR A CHANGE
6-28-95

You ninny!! It's **Angola**!!! Not **Angela**!! "**Angola** Offers Rebel Leader Vice Presidency"!!

©Phil (A TYPOCHONDRIAC) Frank
Should I send out a press release that says "Ignore last press release."?
CRASH

HILDA IS TAKING A GRILLING AT A PUBLIC MAYORAL DEBATE:
Isn't it true that you've **never** held political office before **and** that bears aren't even allowed, technically, to reside in San Francisco?
Well...uh yes, that's true!
MODERATOR

Is it not **also** true that you have poor eyesight?
All bears have weak eyesight... **but** I have an incredible sense of smell!
MODERATOR
6-29-95

And **how**, do tell, would a good sense of smell help you run City Hall?
I can smell rats and dead fish at 300 yards.
MODERATOR
©Phil (ALL ROADS LEAD TO AROMA) Frank

Well... that's it for me. The bear's got **my** vote.
'Scuse me.

IT'S JULY 4TH AND, AS PART OF THE CHRONICLE'S ANNUAL FESTIVITIES, MAYORAL CANDIDATES ADDRESS THE CROWD:
You're on next, Hilda.
But, Farley... there are thousands of people out there!
I can't do it!!
7-4-95

Don't worry. Think of what your political hero would say.
AND NOW... THE ANIMAL RIGHTS CANDIDATE... BRUIN HILDA!!
Okay...

LOOKING OUT UPON THIS SEA OF FACES I AM REMINDED OF THE WORDS OF ANOTHER GREAT AMERICAN...
ICH BIN EIN BERLINER!!
? ? ? ?? ?
©Phil (DRESSED TO THE NEINS) Frank
It worked SO well for Kennedy in '63....
Come on. I'll buy you a hot dog.

MAYORAL CANDIDATE BRUIN HILDA, DEPRESSED BY HER CURRENT POLITICAL STATUS, TAKES A TIP FROM DIANNE FEINSTEIN:
Sigh.
Kitty's Hairdo Pal
OPEN

I'm Hilda. I called about getting my hair colored and getting a full body perm.
Oh!
7-7-95

That's a problem. Our dip tank is out of order. You might try someone who dyes carpets.
©Phil (SHE'S A NAIR-DO-WELL) Frank
I hope for your sake you never need a permit in this town, honey!!

LOOK AT THIS!
Roberta Achtenberg has just released four position papers!!
HILDA
FUR A CHANGE
8-2-95

One on city finances, one on city management, one to form a council of neighborhoods and one to push the city to tackle environmental problems!

SO THAT'S THE WAY SHE WANTS TO PLAY THE GAME...EH?
Lower the level of the campaign...
©Phil (LET'S CALL IT QUIPS) Frank

SHE WANTS TO DISCUSS ISSUES!
Does that mean no swimsuit competition?

Hilda... what's a mayoral campaign without an official campaign song? I've written one!
Oh, great!
8-16-95
Uh one and a two... and a three and a four.
Oh... she looks pretty mean the first time she's seen... All covered up with dark furry hair... But I'd never vote for another. Ooooooooo! Since I saw her standin' there!
© Phil (THE SHRILLS) Frank
Oh... she knows how to cook and catch fish without a hook. Although she could use a little Nair. But I'd never vote for another. Ooooooo! Since I saw her standin' therrre!!
Get the hook!

Tourist Training Camp
Having followed enough slow-moving sightseers in rented vehicles with maps unfolded, hands pointing out windows, and a string of local drivers stuck behind them, I became convinced that there had to be some location where these folks were trained to act and drive the way they do.

San Francisco TOURIST TRAINING CAMP
Now listen up! If you're going to **be** tourists, you're going to **drive** like tourists. Is that clear??
YES, SIR!!
8-8-95
What's **this** driver doing?
SIR!! The car is traveling at the speed limit in the right hand lane.
WHAT IS THE CORRECT PROCEDURE?
SIR! He should be at or below 10 miles per hour, straddling two lanes, backing up traffic for at least one block!
© Phil (THE BOLD, THE FEW, THE LOST) Frank
VERY GOOD! WHAT'S OUR MOTTO?
SIGNAL RIGHT. TURN LEFT!!

I want to see more U-turns on the Golden Gate Bridge!!

YES, SIR!!

© Phil (LOW PODIUM DIET) Frank

When the first humans crossed the land bridge from Asia during the last Ice Age my ancestors ate your ancestors!

Next question?

HILDA READS THE CHRONICLE HEADLINE AND IS DEEPLY TROUBLED:
WHAT? What is this city coming to? ALPHONSE!!
YO!
GIANTS

10-11-95
Send two of our super pizzas to each of the mayoral candidates with my compliments.
Uh... WHY?

WHY? Read the headline!!
?
©Phil (THE GOOD. THE BAD. THE ANCHOVIES.) Frank
S.F. CAMPAIGN: No Pizzazz
Well... English is her second language.

In response to your question... NO... I have never received campaign donations from the tobacco industry or any other special interest group.
BRUIN HILD
FUR A CHANG

10-12-95
Any other group? Any group like... The California Honey Board...or Beekeepers of the Bay Area?
Uh... well...
ACHTENBERG

Are you willing to raise your right paw and swear you are not beholden to any private interest group?
©Phil (A TALON SEARCH) Frank

Um... could I use my left paw?
HILDA
R A CHANGE
HONEY

HILDA PRESSES THE FLESH:
"THE LEAGUE OF MOVIE VOTERS"
NOW PLAYING: DEATH WISH PART VIII
What would you like from your mayor?
A large buttered popcorn.

10-17-95
"MULTI-CULTURAL MUNI SURVIVORS ASSOCIATION"
Okay... So you want ejection seats on every bus... Anything else?

"GOLDEN GATE SAVE YOUR BREATH SOCIETY"
We need Change!!
WE CAN'T HEAR YOU!!

©Phil (STERN MEASURES REQUIRED) Frank
"THE SOCIETY FOR THE NAUTICALLY IMPAIRED":
Your organization has been a mainstay... Get it? Mainstay...
Here comes the Coast Guard!

BRUIN HILDA
FUR A CHANGE
There've been many revelations about your past since the former head ranger at Asphalt State Park has been located.

10-19-95
Horace Malone... that sleazeball, desk-bound bureaucrat!! He couldn't tell the difference between a manzanita bush and a mynah, much less one bear from another in a dumpster...

Do you know the individual referred to?
I do and I...uh... have... the highest respect for... this former director... of...

© Phil (TAIL OF TWO PSYCHES) Frank
ARGH!! I really am becoming a politician!
My client appears overwhelmed by her memories. Let's take five.

HILDA CONTINUES TO POUT ABOUT ANGELA ALIOTO THROWING HER SUPPORT TO ACHTENBERG:
Hilda... it's Angela again...
I don't want to talk to her!

10-23-95
Angela... she's very upset... I know, I know... yes... but... The wrath of a woman bear spurned... well...
GRRRRRR

Well... I think she's learned an important political lesson out of...
GIVE ME THAT PHONE!

© Phil (BITE THE BALLOT) Frank
Here's a political lesson for you, Angela..."Never get between a mother bear and her votes!!"

THE TENSION OF THE CAMPAIGN RUNS HIGH IN THREE OF THE MAYORAL CANDIDATES' CAMPS... BUT IN BRUIN HILDA'S:
We're now into the last week, Hilda! NOW we make the big push!!
I'm list... en... ing...

11-1-95
Here's our campaign wrap-up slogan!!
WHEN YOU CARE ENOUGH TO ELECT THE VERY BEAST!
HILDA?
zzz

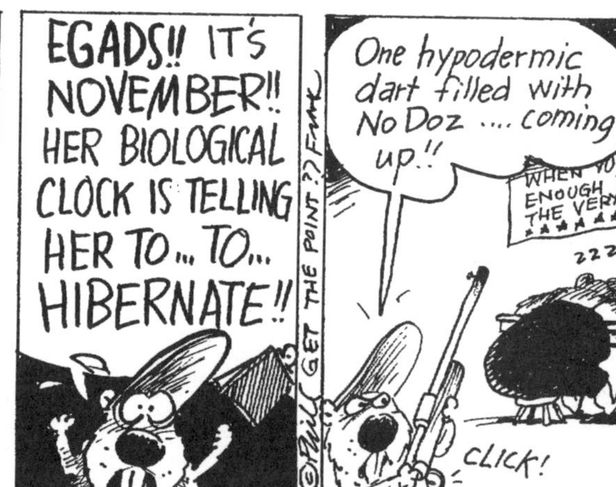
EGADS!! IT'S NOVEMBER!! HER BIOLOGICAL CLOCK IS TELLING HER TO... TO... HIBERNATE!!
© Phil (GET THE POINT?) Frank
One hypodermic dart filled with No Doz .... coming up!!
WHEN YOU CARE ENOUGH TO THE VERY B
zzzz
CLICK!

WIRED ON HOURLY INJECTIONS OF SLEEP DEPRIVATION DRUGS, THE MAYORAL CANDIDATE ATTEMPTS TO MEET THE VOTERS WHILE STAVING OFF HIBERNATION:
So glad to see you. Hope I'll have your vote next week... So good to...
HILDA!! Over here!!

You haven't got a chance of winning!
Thank you! I appreciate your support!

11-2-95
I think it'll be a runoff between Achtenberg and Jordan!
I'll work to improve relations between both Jordan **and** Egypt!
©Phil Frank (A LITTLE SLIGHT OF MIND)
You're going to lie right down to the wire!
Yes... I think I **will** lie down right here...
Time for your medicine, Hilda!

TUESDAY, NOVEMBER 7th. THE BEARS VOTE EARLY AND HEAD FOR THE **FOG CITY DUMPSTER'S** HIBERNATION DEN:
YAWNNNN
INCOMING!
11-7-95

Feels great to get out of this campaign dress and this six-cup Wonderbra!

Hilda... don't you want to hear the election results? What if you won?
©Phil Frank (YAWN OF A NEW ERA)
If I've won tell everyone in City Hall that I'm in a very important meeting. See you in April!

FORMER MAYORAL CANDIDATE BRUIN HILDA IS AWAKENED IN HER HIBERNATION DEN:
KNOCK! KNOCK!
HUNH? WASS THAT?

12-11-97
Hilda!! We finally got the count on the write-in votes from the Registrar!!
Oh?

You got fifteen votes.
Fifteen votes? You woke me to tell me I got fifteen votes?
©Phil Frank (A LEGEND IN HER OWN MIND)
The Registrar said that was pretty good. The official write-in candidate only got one vote.
Oh. So am I the mayor?

I never look forward to this conversation...
Bruce?
Yes?
11-22-95

Will you be joining Irene and Olive and me for Thanksgiving dinner tomorrow?
Time for the annual turkey murder? As a fellow avian I must decline!

What will **you** do?
I'll be joining a large group of my scavenger friends for a gathering out at the Farallon Islands for our own Thanksgiving dinner.
© Phil Frank FOOD FOR THOUGHT
Word has it a dead whale has washed ashore.
Well... to each his own...

DAY AFTER THANKSGIVING LEFTOVERS OUT ON THE FARALLON ISLANDS.
We'll **never** finish this thing.
Soup! We'll make soup!
11-24-95

I love the holidays... don't you?
Oh no! Alice is here with those three bratty kids!

Sonar experiments in Monterey Bay. Three dead whales in three weeks. Coincidence? I think not.
Don't be an alarmist!
© Phil Frank I'LL HAVE A BYTE

Tell me... how'd you find out about this?
Like most every bird here... on the Internet.

You know, Orwell... I'm really gonna miss Calvin and Hobbes. That's my idea of humor!
You kind of remind me of Hobbes, the tiger, Speedbump.
12-28-95

Funny... **you** remind **me** of Calvin, the egocentric, conniving little kid!
Really? I'm honored.

Orwell... **we** could draw a cartoon about our funny lives here in Golden Gate Park. We could call it "**Speedbump and Orwell**".
Give me **one** reason to do that!
© Phil Frank GET THE LEAD OUT
Um.. 2400 newspapers looking for a replacement strip.
Hand me that pencil and paper.

My wife Susan and I went to see **Don Giovanni** at the Opera House, and as I watched the actors on the stage, I easily envisioned our political candidates in their own little opera.

Wriggletto (The Whole Thing Makes Me Squirm) is, I think, my tour de force with real and pretend Italian. It was fun to create but the process left me totally exhausted.

THE CURTAIN RISES AS COUNT BRIONI-FERRARI, PLAYED BY BARITONE WILLIE BROWN, ENTERS:

12-5-95

THE PAYMENTS FROM DEVELOPERS, TOBACCO FIRMS AND LEGAL CLIENTS CONTINUE TO HAUNT THE COUNT, WEIGHING HEAVY IN THE SYMBOLIC FORM OF BAGGAGE. ENTER THE SPECTRE.

YOU AGAIN?

CASTING ASIDE THE BAGGAGE FERRARI PLACES A HANDKERCHIEF UPON THE STAGE SO THAT HE MAY KNEEL WITHOUT SOILING HIS SUIT. HE SINGS THE LAMENT: "Why do you harass me so? I am but a humble attorney."

©PHIL (WILLIE DO IT?) FRANK

SECRETLY NURSING PLANS OF REVENGE UPON THE FEW MEMBERS OF THE PRESS WHO HAVE NOT GIVEN HIM THE ADORATION HE FEELS HE DESERVES, HE MAKES A LIST:

ONE... TWO... THREE... FOUR

Act III
"Wriggletto"
("THE WHOLE THING MAKES ME SQUIRM")

THE CURTAIN RISES ON THE **MAYOR DOMO**, PLAYED BY TENOR FRANK JORDAN, GARBED IN A SHOWER CURTAIN, WAVING A BATH BRUSH.

12-6-95

IN THE BACKGROUND, THE HEAD OF HIS PALACE GUARD, PLAYED BY BARITONE TONY RIBERA, IS INVOLVED IN A PUBLIC YELLING MATCH WITH HIS FORMER ASSISTANT, PLAYED BY SOPRANO JOANNE WELSH. THE MAYOR CRIES OUT:

Perche adesso per deo's cara

WHY **NOW**, FOR GOD'S SAKE?

HE THEN CLIMBS TO THE PALACE TOWER AND SINGS HIS LAMENT:

Ho ecce betrada!! Mi retinute partire me... Solo esparanza es mi popolo

I AM BETRAYED. MY SUPPORTERS ABANDON ME. MY ONLY HOPE IS MY PEOPLE.

©Phil (MUSSOLINI DID IT?) Frank

HE SINGS TO THE PEOPLE WAITING IN THE PUBLIC SQUARE: "My record is clean. I work hard for you. Vote for me."

Mi recordo es pulice...

Ha! Il duce buono fare autobuses muni prompto!

HA! A GOOD LEADER MAKES THE BUSES RUN ON TIME!

Act IV
"Wriggletto"
("THE WHOLE THING MAKES ME SQUIRM")

THE CURTAIN RISES AS THE MAYOR DOMO (PLAYED BY TENOR FRANK JORDAN) DESCENDS INTO THE CAVERN BENEATH THE CIVIC PALACE.

ACT V
"Wriggletto"
("THE WHOLE THING MAKES ME SQUIRM")
THE CURTAIN RISES ON A CHAMBER OF THE PALACE WHICH IS CURRENTLY UNDERGOING EARTHQUAKE REPAIRS.
12-8-95

USING FANS TO CONCEAL THEIR IDENTITIES, THE CONSPIRING SISTERS ANGELA AND ROBERTA (PLAYED BY ANGELA AND ROBERTA) PLOT TO UNSEAT THE MAYOR DOMO (PLAYED BY TENOR FRANK JORDAN).
KNOCK!! KNOCK!!

THEY WILL TRADE THEIR VOTES TO COUNT BRIONI-FERRARI (PLAYED BY WILLIE BROWN) FOR HIS SUPPORT WHEN THEY RUN FOR OFFICE. THE COUNT SIGNS THE STIPULATED AGREEMENT AND SINGS:
Peree tutto essere in tre plicate?
MUST EVERYTHING BE IN TRIPLICATE?

IN THE BALCONY SCENE, THE SISTERS ADDRESS THE ASSEMBLED CONSTRUCTION WORKERS AND SUPPORTERS:
Noi ricevere... in scrivere!!
SORELLA UNITO
SISTERS UNITED
WE GOT IT IN WRITING!
©Phil Frank TUNE IN SUNDAY!
MEANWHILE, IN AN ADJOINING ROOM THE MAYOR DOMO LAMENTS:
Non mi sento bene.
I DON'T FEEL SO GOOD.

This is the final act of the 1995 San Francisco political opera season's stirring production of Machiavelli's
"Wriggletto"
("THE WHOLE THING MAKES ME SQUIRM.")
AS THE CURTAIN RISES, THE ENTIRE CAST SLOWLY GATHERS ON THE STAGE FOR THE FINALE:
12-10-95

THE MAYOR DOMO, PLAYED BY TENOR FRANK JORDAN, ENTERS WRAPPED IN A SHOWER CURTAIN FOLLOWED CLOSELY BY HIS WIFE, THE POWER BEHIND HIS THRONE. HE LAMENTS HIS SUPPORTERS' DEFECTIONS:
Io sono giu... ingrati...
I GOT THOSE UNGRATEFUL CONSTITUENT BLUES...

ENTERING STAGE RIGHT, CARRYING MUCH POLITICAL BAGGAGE AND WISHING HE WERE IN THE ROLE OF OTHELLO IS COUNT BRIONI-FERRARI, PLAYED BY WILLIE BROWN. HE TOO IS SINGING:
Non piangiare per me, Sacramento
DON'T CRY FOR ME, SACRAMENTO.

ENTER NOW THEIR POLITICAL ADVISERS, PLAYED BY CLINT REILLY AND JACK DAVIS. THEY CARRY BUCKETS OF MUD AND BAGS OF SILVER AND SING AS THEY PASS THE CHIEF OF THE PALACE GUARD (TONY RIBERA) AND HIS FORMER ASSISTANT (SOPRANO JOANNE WELSH).
Le cose che facciamo per i soldi
THE THINGS WE DO FOR MONEY.

ENTER NOW THE DANCING HOMELESS PERFORMING THE TOUCHING "TARANTELLA de MATRIX." THEY ARE FOLLOWED CLOSELY BY THE PALACE GUARD. THE HOMELESS DO THE HARVEST DANCE AND SING WHILE THE CONSPIRING SISTERS, ANGELA AND ROBERTA, LOOK ON:
Quanta costa allumino oggi.
WHAT'S THE PRICE OF ALUMINUM TODAY?

FINALLY... THE SQUABBLING SIBLINGS FAZIO AND HALLINAN ENTER, SWORDS DRAWN:
CLACK! CLACK!
CLACK! CLACK!
©Phil Frank (WHERE DID WE FAIL THEM?)

THEY ALL JOIN THE CHORUS, PLAYED BY THE BOARD OF SUPERVISORS, AND SING IN TOTAL DISHARMONY THE TOUCHING FINALE:
Mama... Non far creiere i tuoi bambini ad essere politici!!
"MAMA, DON'T LET YOUR KIDS GROW UP TO BE POLITICIANS"

I saw the headline in the **Chronicle** - "Another House Demo Becomes a Republican" - and immediately envisioned a clinic somewhere... probably in a conservative part of Southern California... where Democrats are taken to undergo this tricky operation.

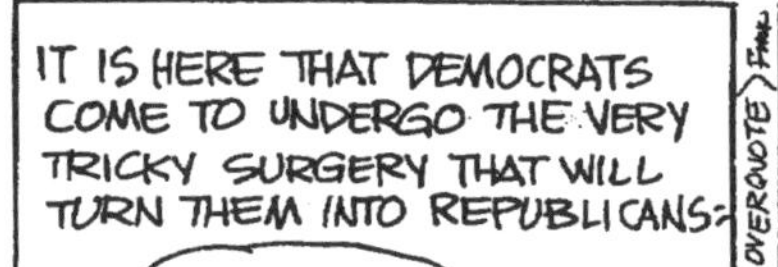

Farley continues to daydream after reading the headline:
Another House Demo Becomes a Republican
Where... am... I...?
You're in the recovery room at the Jerry Ford Clinic, Representative Erstwhile...
zzzzz
1-24-96
I... must... get... up... I'm... needed... in Washington...
Tax... breaks for... the... wealthy...
States... rights...
Quash... Medicare...
Stop... the... summer... job... program...
Down... with... daycare...
Bust... the... unions...
THEY'RE KILLING THE ENTITLEMENTS!!
Whoa, Farley. Better lay off the caffeine...
© Phil (BREW HA HA) Frank

Farley's headline-induced daydream continues:
Another House Demo Becomes a Republican

He is assisting in the recovery room at the JERRY FORD CLINIC in Palm Springs where many former Democrats are in post-op.
Sir... sir... how are you feeling?
NNNH...
zzzzz
1-25-96

Did... the oper..a..tion... work?
We don't know yet, Representative. Would you like some water?
© Phil (I'LL DRINK TO THAT) Frank

Water... YES!!...Water! Give the commercial growers all the water they need!! What's good for agri-biz is good for America!!
Apparently the operation was a success...

The San Francisco Zoo's VALENTINE'S DAY SEX TOUR is under way.
Leaving the primates we now come to our amorous birds...
2-14-96

On your right you will see one of our male peacocks beginning his courtship ritual.
WOW!

He has spread his fan and is fluttering it to attract a female to mate.
Good work, pal!
© Phil (IT'S IN THE JEANS) Frank

The females are, as usual, disinterested... so he is now displaying for... a... fire hydrant!
Just like a man!

It seemed to me that every disenfranchised group in San Francisco had its supporters and political action committee. In every article I read about MUNI's problems someone would mention the cockroaches—but no one stood up for the little buggers. Many of them, I was sure, were just commuters, heading to their jobs in upscale pantries. I stepped forward as their defender.

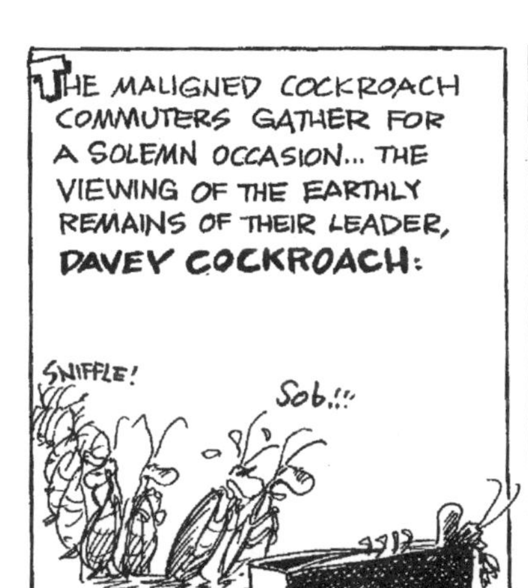

SUDDENLY... THE MOURNERS FREEZE AS THE CORPSE RISES:

!!!

Sat on by an attorney? It takes more than that to kill a cockroach!!

Willie Brown, the city's new mayor, was shooting from the lip with some of his ideas: Let the homeless camp in the city parks! Nobody liked that idea so Willie backed up and said what he **really** meant was that **anyone** could camp in the parks. I liked the idea of Willie doing a little urban camping.

WILLIE AND HIS SPIRITUAL ADVISER ARE OFF ON AN URBAN ADVENTURE... CAMPING:
Golden Gate Park... and step on it!
Yes, sir...

3-19-96
Any particular part of the park, Mister Mayor?
Some place with trees and no people.

Where are we?
Near the buffalo enclosure, sir.
Ah... what an aroma!
© Phil (HE SAID, INTENTLY) Frank

I feel just like John Muir, Baba!
I don't think he had a suede tent from Wilkes Bashford...

IN A SUEDE TENT PURCHASED FROM WILKES BASHFORD, THE MAYOR, AS URBAN CAMPER, INITIATES HIS ADVISER INTO THE JOYS OF CAMPING IN A CITY PARK:
I enjoyed that hike today, Baba.
The Municipal Golf Course never looked so good.
CAMP WILLIE

3-20-96
I really worked up an appetite... Speaking of which... I think we forgot to pack dinner.
I've got trail mix and dried apple rings...

I was thinking more along the lines of won ton soup, spicy prawn black bean chow fun and green tea ice cream.
You haven't camped much, have you?
© Phil (DIALING FOR DIM SUM) Frank

Man!... this is **urban** camping! Get it? I know a place on Irving that delivers! Give me my cellular phone!

IT'S THE MORNING AFTER AT "CAMP WILLIE" IN GOLDEN GATE PARK:
I don't know about this urban camping experience, Baba. I was really scared last night.
Oh?
3-21-96

The backfiring MUNI buses weren't too bad... and I could live with the strange noises outside the tent... and even the car alarm on Fulton Street.
What was it then?

Never should have ordered that spicy Chinese food and had it delivered.
Let me guess... scary dream?
Real scary.
© Phil (ONE WEDDING AND A FUNERAL) Frank

I had to officiate at the wedding of Jack Davis and Rose Pak. Ohhh...
That **is** scary.

Here it is...
HAND ME THE SEAT!
3-22-96

AT THE MUNI RAILWAY HEADQUARTERS ON PRESIDIO THE FIRST OF MANY SPECIAL SEATS ARE BEING INSTALLED FOLLOWING A CLASS-ACTION LAWSUIT...
DRILL!
Drill.

...A SUIT FILED ON BEHALF OF THE MALIGNED COCKROACH COMMUTERS OF SAN FRANCISCO:
Members of the press... the individual who fought for what he believed... Davey Cockroach.
©Phil (LITTLE BIG MAN) Frank

WE MAY BE SMALL...BUT WE HAVE RIGHTS TOO!
WHAT DID HE SAY?

David Letterman was coming to San Francisco to do his show. Jeesh! You'd think the pope was coming. Hype and hooplah! Huzzah... huzzah!! I thought Baba's fax machine would serve well for a little reader interaction. Baba and I got swamped with material.
BZZT!
BZZT!
BZZT!!
BZZT!!

BABA'S FAX MACHINE AND E-MAIL GO INTO WARP SPEED AS SUGGESTIONS FOR "THE TOP 10 REASONS DAVID LETTERMAN SHOULD COME TO SAN FRANCISCO" POUR IN:
YIKES!!
BZZZP!
BZZZP!
BZZZP!
BZZZP!
2-27-96
City's supervisors perform "Stupid Pet Tricks" daily... Dan Beaver
FAX: 415-332-6900 E-MAIL: guru@well.com
We don't bother to import French wine... We import French toilets... Karl Wonn.
©Phil (HAIR TODAY GONE TOMALES) Frank
Lee Glickstein writes: Paul Shaffer could do a reprise of that old favorite "I Left My Hair in San Francisco."

The Official Top Ten Reasons Why David Letterman should Bring His Show to San Francisco:

10. He can hail a cab here without waving a weapon!
9. He is single and straight and Angela Alioto is available and looking.
8. We put the "Wah?" in "Wahoo"!
7. To earn some extra cash he can be a moist towel valet at our new pay toilets!
6. He can improve his jogging by running through the Tenderloin wearing a t-shirt that says: "I'm a Celebrity and I'm Carrying Big Wads of Cash!"

3-6-96

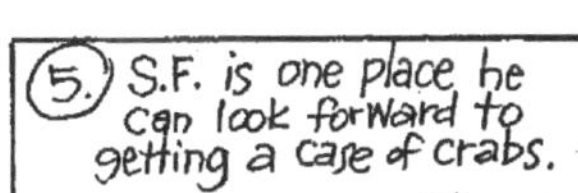

5. S.F. is one place he can look forward to getting a case of crabs.
4. New York has D'Amato. We have Da Mayor.
3. If he has a show as bad as the Oscars, the Golden Gate Bridge is handy.
2. He is outside the jurisdiction of the Connecticut State Police.

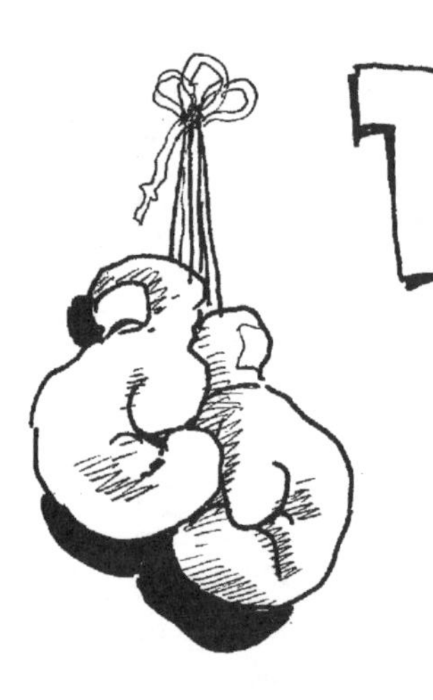

Terence Hallinan, our newly elected district attorney and former boxer, seemed to be getting himself into hot water every time he turned around. The culmination was a sparring match with residential developer Joe O'Donoghue.

Someone needed to look into the allegations. What crimefighter would be better than...uh... the district attorney?

The District Attorney is very upset that the media has chosen to use innuendo, rumors and half-truths about this incident involving him and Joe O'Donoghue!
I see.
5-6-96

Terence is anxious to defend himself against these scurrilous allegations!
Great.

And in the far corner, wearing red trunks and weighing 165..is the "Battling D.A." defending his title ... the hometown kid...KAYO... HALLINAN!!
©Phil (BOB AND WEAVE) Frank

THE D.A.'s TACTIC WAS UNUSUAL..BUT AFTER ALL... THIS IS SAN FRANCISCO:
I know this is difficult for you... but tell the court in your own words exactly what happened...
5-13-96

I don't know... the election went so well.. Then the pink slip dismissal debacle... Then the sexual harassment charge... Then the birthday party dust-up...

But, Mr. Hallinan... isn't it true you went to the police... you wanted to press the matter against Joe O'Donoghue?
It's true...but I realize now that it was a desperate action. I was confused.. angry...
©Phil (CAN I GET BACK TO YOU?) Frank

Clearly you were confused... in fact weren't you a victim of your own imaginings? Is that not true, Mr. Hallinan?
WELL?

A WHITE BMW WITH VANITY PLATES PLOWS THROUGH A WILDFLOWER PATCH. THE DRIVER IS TALKING ON HIS CAR PHONE:
Hello, Millie...
RRRRRMM!!
S.F. Water De Reservoir

It's Fred here! Gads!! It's beautiful out here in the watershed! Let's close up the firm for the summer.
6-5-96

Sounds good, Mister Dally. What do I do about the clients in the waiting room?
DILLY DALLY DOLITTLE & STAHL ATTORNE AT LAW
©Phil (RESERVOIR HOGS) Frank
Take... deposits... tell clients... we're...working... on their...cases... Pick up... Margarita mix... meet you... at Crystal Springs reservoir...
Got it.

LIKE THE SWALLOWS RETURNING TO CAPISTRANO, THE FERAL PIGS HAVE RETURNED TO BAY AREA RESERVOIRS.
SLEEPY WALLOW
FERALDO!
ZZZZZZ
SNORK!
6-6-96

What is it, my tender pork rind?
Look who's coming.

It's Sybil and Steve Swineson with their obnoxious brood in their new Land Crusher.
HI, SYBIL!!
©Phil (BEAST OF FRIENDS) Frank

Now we're going to have to listen to him prattle on about his new luber rooter from Shar-pei Image...
The man is a total boar!

5-31-96
AROOOOOOOOOO
Prom night for all the obedience schools.
FOG CITY DUMP
©Phil (MUZZLE TOF!) Frank

Goose .. party of two!!
FOG CITY DUMPSTER

What's the Chef's pâté?
Well...
6-13-96

An unemployed chef is force-fed grain until his liver is one-fourth the size of his body. At that point..
©Phil (TAKE A GANDER) Frank

I'll have the garden salad and an iced tea.
Good choice.

The further adventures of Orwell T. Catt:
The Clintons are being bombarded with incriminating paperwork. If only some staff member's prints could be found on the papers, the White House would have a scapegoat... or scapecat, as the case might be.

ORWELL T. CATT GETS HIS INTRODUCTION TO THE TWENTY-NINE PALMS FEDERAL PET-ITENTIARY FROM THE WARDEN, BILLY JOE PECKINPAW:
You're not the first celebrity we've ever had in here, Catt.
7-17-96

You say you're innocent of handling all those White House files... that you're just a scapecat...
Well, boy... ah don't much care.
To me... you're just another prisoner.

Keep your nose clean, follow the rules and we'll get along just fine. Any questions?
Can I get my canned tuna fish in spring water instead of oil?
© Phil (The Scales of Justice) Frank

CLANG!
Tuna fish in oil it is!

ORWELL IS CURRENTLY INCARCERATED AT THE TWENTY-NINE PALMS FEDERAL PET-ITENTIARY:
Yeah... I did it!! Those are my paw prints on all those White House files. But it was all a set-up. What about you?
I'm Harold Stassen's dog.

Harold Stassen? Isn't he the 89-year-old eternal Republican candidate for president? Didn't he volunteer to be Bob Dole's running mate?
Yeah... that's my owner.
7-18-96

I didn't know it's a federal crime to be his dog.
It's not but I guess what I did is a crime.
So... what did you do?
I buried his hairpiece in the garden.
© Phil (Toupee or not toupee: that is the question) Frank

What was that on his head in the newspaper photos?
It was a CIA-drugged squirrel.

In national news... The House Committee on Government Reform and Oversight gave notice of the expansion of their investigation into drug use at the White House...
...to include the Clinton pets!
7-22-96

I was the special agent in charge. There were many times I saw the former head of feline security, one Orwell T. Catt, supply Socks with hallucinogens...
Can you be more specific?

CATNIP. You'd see the two of them in their offices with glazed stares, chasing dust balls, hanging from the Oval Office curtains, attacking balls of Hillary's knitting yarn.
It was pretty sick.
Back to you, Brad.
© Phil (Creature of Halibut) Frank

Orwell T. Catt is presently incarcerated at a federal pet-itentiary. He is serving a ten-year sentence. Unfortunately, that's in dog years...

ORWELL T. CATT GETS A VISITOR AT THE FEDERAL PET-ITENTIARY:
SPEEDBUMP!! MY MAN!
Hi, Orwell.
7-23-96
So... tell me, Orwell... How are you doing?
Can't complain. The food's okay... They change my litter gravel every other day... I'm reading a lot...
What I mean is... how are you doing emotionally? Have you seen the error of your ways? Have you found God yet? You **are** wearing a prison number on your shirt, you know...
You're right and that reminds me...
©Phil (LOTTO LUCK!) Frank
Here's a buck. Can you play my number on the lottery?
Well... that answers that...

AT THE FEDERAL PET-ITENTIARY:
What's the news from Frisco, Speedbump?
CalTrans'll start tearing down the Central Freeway soon... Mel Belli died... Willie's still doin' his thing...
7-24-96

Do you have enough money for snacks and such, Orwell?
I'm loaded, dude! Check out **this** wad! The warden let me bring in two cases of "**Primary Colors**". I've been signing them "Anonymous" and selling them to the dogs.
Those dudes are **so** dumb!

OH! THAT REMINDS ME!! "Anonymous" has been exposed as Joe Klein... a correspondent for Newsweek. He's admitted it.
So... so... **he's** "Anonymous" and everyone knows? That means that I'm... I'm...
©Phil (BETTER FLED THAN DEAD) Frank
Is "dead" the word you're looking for?
GET ME OUTTA HERE!!

IN A RARE GESTURE OF SUBMISSION, ORWELL T. CATT SEEKS THE HELP OF THE TOP PRISON CAT AT THE **TWENTY-NINE PALMS FEDERAL PET-ITENTIARY**:
A-hem! ER... Sam? Sam Quentin?
YEAH? WHAT IS IT?
8-2-96

There's been a big mistake. I shouldn't be in *here*!! I was used as a scapecat by the Democrats. I must get out!
Why should I help **you**?

There's a gang of dogs in here that want to ice *me*!
Well... I could talk to the guards... get you an outdoors job... but it'll cost you... BIG!
© Phil (THE CAT'S PAJAMAS) Frank
I could maybe arrange for you to take care of the warden's pet birds.
Oh. **That** would be nice.

I owe this one to Herb Caen and to Mayor Willie Brown's imperial style. When Herb dubbed the Mayor "His Williness" it seemed perfect to take it one step further... Put him in ermine robes... give him a crown a scepter and his own private sedan chair (**MUNI 1**) carried by four soldiers of his private guard. Lastly, let the Mayor Domo live in the marbled rooms of City Hall.

Tell me, Mirror... What do you think about this possible trade... Treasure Island for the Headwaters Forest in Humboldt County?
Well...

7-30-96
Treasure Island **is** a prime location with many potential uses... housing, movie studios and a major theme park...
True...

Yet its problems are large. It is sinking, needs immense financing to make everything happen. If you trade it for the Forest these headaches will not be **your** headaches!
Hmm...
© Phil (Statute of Limitations) Frank
Thou wouldst gain immeasurable respect in Washington, future chits and a bronze statue of your highness put up somewhere.
I like the way this mirror thinks...

Hail, Prince of the Western Slopes and the Pacific Plate... You alone are one Potent tate!
Okay... okay... Knock off all the platitudes, Mirror. I need your help!

8-19-96
You've got to help me get that gator out of Mountain Lake in the Presidio!
Oh?

Pray tell... Why is an alligator in a city park so important to capture?
Because, you ninny...
That dude is gettin' more press than I am!
© Phil (Later, Gator) Frank
NOW... ONE SHOT WITHOUT THE CAP!
DA GATOR

There is only **one** individual I know who can lure that gator from the lake and turn the media attention back to you, sire.
SPEAK! SPEAK!

He is the former head of the Steinhart Aquarium.
GOOD CREDENTIALS!!
Unfortunately he's presently incarcerated.
I'll get him out!!

8-20-96
He is Orwell T. Catt... former head of Feline Security for "Socks".
Perfect! Clinton owes me **big**... and I know **just** the attorney!!

© Phil (It's a Flea-Bargain) Frank
AN HOUR LATER AT **29 PALMS FEDERAL PET-ITENTIARY:**
I want to see the warden. Tell him Flea Bailey is here with a pardon from the President!
ITCH! ITCH!

The Summer Olympics were in full swing with all their hype, hoopla, star worship and product endorsement contracts.

Why shouldn't a version of all that be taking place out in the woods? It could be the **1996 State Park Summer Olympics**.

FARLEY FILES HIS DAILY REPORT FROM THE SITE OF THE STATE PARK SUMMER OLYMPICS:
Today the men's freestyle wrestling competition was held...
Phone
ASPHALT STATE PARK

It was no surprise when the first place gold medal went to the perennial favorite, a local boy. He won by default.
7-15-96

He won by default?
Correct.
(WITH A NAME LIKE SMACKERS...)

GRRRRR...
WHOA!! THE PEANUT BUTTER'S YOURS, DUDE!

FARLEY SITS IN THE PRESS BOX AT THE STATE PARK SUMMER OLYMPICS:
What a day it's been here, folks. Let's re-cap the day's events as we bask in the glow of the park's Olympic barbecue.
WELCOME TO ASPHALT STATE PARK

"Helen Cleaverdyke, an Orinda housewife, came from behind to take a gold in the women's 800 meter nature speed walk..."
STELLAR JAY ON A DECAYING CONIFER... MIOCENE EPOCH VOLCANIC FORMATIONS ON THE LEFT...
7-19-96

"Dan Ostrander, a cable TV installer, set a new park record of 152 feet, 4 inches in the men's discus using a standard 18" pizza tin from Pizza Cabin, official pizza to the State Park Summer Olympics:"

"And lastly, in the finals of the 4-man canoe competition, a quartet of computer nerds from Chico beat out the highly touted but somewhat overweight local team."
FINISH
(THE AGONY OF WET FEET)

FARLEY FILES HIS REPORT FOR THE PAPER ON THE STATE PARK SUMMER OLYMPICS:
"In Track and Field... once again the most popular event...
Phone
ASPHALT STATE PARK

"...was the Couples' 200 meter Restroom Relay won by the Andersons of Laguna Honda..."

"There was strong competition in the Men's Beer Can Toss... a difficult sport... Close is important here. You get it in...you lose."

KEEP OUR PARK CLEAN
(GOLDEN STATE WORRIER)

"But, of course, the most popular event today was the Get Drunk and Do Something Really Stupid Freestyle competition."

Many campers are pinning their hopes, dreams and bets on one athlete... Velma Melmac, who is representing the U.S. in the 100-yard Nature Trail Clean and Clear Competition.

NO SMOKING

8-1-96

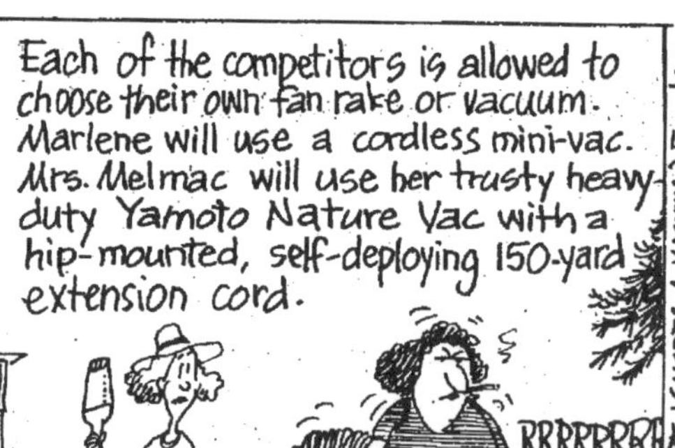

And so, once again, the curtain falls on another amazing State Park Summer Olympics...
It was a truly touching moment at last night's closing ceremonies...
8-5-96

...when the Olympic Barbecue, which had burned so brightly for two weeks, was snuffed out.

The athletes are busy packing up and pulling out... Let's have one last word with our gold medal winner, Velma Melmac of Manteca...

What will you do with **your** gold medal, Velma?
I'm going to have it bronzed.
Really, what else is there to say? From the 1996 State Park Summer Olympics... Good day.
©Phil (GO FOR THE BRONZE!) Frank

Thy countenance doth sour, sire. Art thou not pleased with the latest poll in the supervisors' race, exalted one?
We are **not** amused!!
10-8-96

This former hooker, Margo St. James hath good numbers, but she owes me no allegiance!!
But...thou endorsed her, sire!
That's when I thought her candidacy was a joke, ninny! Find out what you can about her!
I FLY LIKE THE WIND, SIRE!!
©Phil (A ROYAL PAIN IN THE BUTTRESS) Frank
AEIIIII
THUD!
Good help is so hard to find these days...

You sent for me, Sire?
Some Royal Reptile Catcher you turned out to be!!
10-14-96

A proposed annual budget of $80,000 for a "Wait and Seize" approach to catch one 3-foot-long alligator!

An on-site observation post at Mountain Lake with a staff rec room, pool table, hot tub, CD player, jet-ski!!!
GULP!
©Phil (WATCH OUT FOR THE COD PIECE) Frank

THEY CAUGHT THE GATOR WITH $1.47 WORTH OF COD!! YOU'RE FIRED!!
May the Blue Angels perform a complicated maneuver in your royal shorts!

Depressed and destitute, Orwell considers jumping from the **Golden Gate Bridge**. The series spun out of demands for an unobtrusive suicide barrier. I rented the Jimmy Stewart film **It's A Wonderful Life**, created a guardian angel cat for Orwell and had fun with the series.

Frank Jordan wouldn't have had an appointee to head the Steinhart Aquarium..."Socks" wouldn't have had a feline security agent... Willie Brown wouldn't have had a gator catcher...

©Phil (GEORGE BAILEY WONTCHA PLEASE COME HOME) Frank

No one will ever collect that money if you're not here to turn in that painted rock!

Remember the Million Cat March on Washington, California... that tiny gold mining town near Nevada City... the march you planned for November?

UPDATE!

DUE TO WANDERING STORY LINES, IT IS OCCASIONALLY NECESSARY TO TRACK CHARACTERS. AS A SERVICE TO OUR READERS.

BABA RE BOK, SIDEWALK PSYCHIC IS STILL RECOVERING FROM HIS DATE WITH LESLIE, THE "SPUNKY BUDDHIST."

BRUCE THE RAVEN, WHO FLEW UP TO THE **HEADWATERS FOREST** TO TAKE PART IN THE SAGA, WAS CAUGHT IN A JOURNALISTIC VACUUM WHEN A TENTATIVE SETTLEMENT WAS WORKED OUT. HE'S STILL THERE... WAITING FOR EDITORIAL DIRECTION.

10-24-96

THE FERAL PIGS WHO INVADED **BLACKHAWK** TO ROOT UP LAWNS AND GARDENS ARE SLEEPING OFF THEIR FEEDING ORGY IN AN EAST BAY CUL DE SAC.

BEPPO, WHO INVESTED ALL HIS MONEY IN A ROLLING CAFE, AND WENT BELLY UP WHEN TRAFFIC GRIDLOCK FAILED TO MATERIALIZE, HAS SOLD OUT TO **STARBUCKS**.

© Phil (TRANSCENDENTAL MEDICATION) Frank

ORWELL T. CATT, WHO WAS CONTEMPLATING FELINICIDE BY JUMPING FROM THE GOLDEN GATE BRIDGE, IS PRESENTLY RESTING COMFORTABLY IN THE PSYCHIATRIC WING OF THE **S.P.C.A.**

Open wide! Insert foot! His Williness really put his foot in it this time... twice in two weeks! The first was an off-handed comment in a television interview in which he derided his Supervisors and the other from Paris in reference to Elvis Grbac's performance as the 49er quarterback.

10-29-96

© Phil SECOND FLOOR... REIGN GEAR? Frank

WITH HIS DRAWBRIDGE RAISED, HIS WILLINESS ATTEMPTS TO MAKE PEACE WITH HIS SUPES:
When I referred to politicians as pantywaists... mistresses that needed to be serviced, I certainly didn't mean you!
RIGHT!

10-29-96
SEND UP ONE REPRESENTATIVE TO DISCUSS THE MATTER.
SEND UP THE ROYAL REPTILE CATCHER!!

STAND BY TO RECEIVE THE ROYAL REPTILE CATCHER!!
Now I see why these things are called catapults!
PA:ZANG

One Exocat missile approaching at a high rate of speed, Sire.
I'll be in the wine cellar.
©Phil (DID HE SAY WHINE CELLAR?) Frank

THE TRADE AND GOODWILL CONTINGENT DEPARTS SFO FOR PARIS. HIS WILLINESS SPEAKS:
As your beloved ruler I bid thee farewell. We travel to the French lands to the east.

There we shall dine in royal splendor and seek the hand of fair Paris as our sister city.
Au revoir.
11-11-96

THE STAIRS ARE ROLLED AWAY FROM THE GETTY JET AS THE ENGINES WHINE AND THE CROWD ROARS THEIR SALUTATIONS.
BON VOYAGE!!
EEEEE
©Phil (LIFE IS A CABERNET) Frank

THE PLANE BEGINS ITS TAXI DOWN THE RUNWAY:
KEEP THE SUPERVISORS OUT OF THE WINE CELLAR!
EEEE

YESTERDAY THE GETTY JET, ARRIVING FROM FRANCE, TAXIED TO A STOP BEFORE A WAITING CROWD AT SFO:
EEEEEEEEE
11-18-96

THE FIRST OFF THE PLANE IS PRESS SECRETARY KANDACE BENDER, WHO, AFTER THE GRBAC FIASCO AND THE NEWS THAT ROME, NOT SAN FRANCISCO, IS PARIS' ACTUAL SISTER CITY, IS SAID TO BE RESTING COMFORTABLY.
OHHHHHH

NEXT... THE MAYOR DOMO EMERGED REFRESHED AND AS USUAL, UPBEAT...
©Phil (A 24 CARROT SETTING) Frank

...AND OBLIVIOUS:
Ah... the citizens have brought me gifts of aged fruit and vegetables...

THE MAYOR DOMO FINDS HIMSELF IN THE ROYAL PRISON OF DISRESPECT:
SLAM!
What are you looking at, rodent?

What fickle winds of fate be these that fill the sails of this, my ship of despair...

...and blow my little craft upon the rocky shores of public contempt? Cease, I say! Cease!
11-19-96

©Phil (QUOTH THE MAVEN...) Frank
"Me howling winds drive devious, tempest toss'd, Sails ript, seams opn'ning wide, and compass lost."
Great... I'm jailed with a rat that quotes William Cowper.

IN THE ROYAL HOLDING CELL:
Lord... it's me... Willie... little Willie Brown from Mineola, Texas...
11-20-96

I've come a long way over the years, Lord... I hope you're proud of your little boy. I know I am!

But I fear that in my quest for power I have at times said arrogant things that have hurt others. I seek thy help in ridding me of my arro...
RING! RING!
©Phil (HOOF-IN-MOUTH DISEASE) Frank

Whoops! There's my cell phone!! Listen, God... just get in touch with my press secretary about all this! 'Bye.
RING!

FREE WILLIE!!
FREE WILLIE!!
FREE WILLIE
FREE WILLIE
Good morning from San Francisco!
1
12-10-96

What looks like a scene from a re-make of a popular film about a whale is actually a rally outside the dungeon beneath City Hall...
FREE WILLIE!!
FREE WILLIE

It is here that the mayor has been kept incarcerated for certain ill-chosen statements. However, pressure from some citizens is allowing the mayor to be given an early release.
It is, afterall, the holiday season.
FREE WILLIE!

HERE HE COMES NOW!! WILLIE!! ANY COMMENT?
DO I HAVE ANY COMMENT?
©Phil (PHLEGM AT ELEVEN) Frank
Er... not at the moment.
Reporting for the Channel One "ONE-EYE NEWS TEAM."...

Mas margaritas, por favor!!

While working on a project for Yosemite National Park, I learned that technically, California black bears don't hibernate; they just take long sleeps. The weather doesn't get snowy enough for them to go into a five-month snooze. So I thought... instead of dozing in a dank den under a restaurant... how about under a palm tree in Puerto Vallarta, Mexico?

THE BEARS HAVE MADE IT TO THEIR HIBERNATION DEN FOR THE WINTER... THE CASUAL BUT COMFORTABLE HOTEL ROSITA IN PUERTO VALLARTA, MEXICO:
Buenos dias.
Buenas tardes.
GIANTS
PINK FLOYD
GOOD DAY.
GOOD AFTERNOON.

11-26-96
Um... Quisiera dos habitaciones con dos camas, por favor.
¿Cuánto tiempo piensa quedarse, señora?
I WOULD LIKE TWO ROOMS WITH TWIN BEDS, PLEASE.
HOW LONG DO YOU INTEND TO STAY, MADAM?

Uh... cuatro meses
¿CUATRO MESES?
FOUR MONTHS.
FOUR MONTHS?
©Phil (IT BEARS WATCHING) Frank
Drat!! There's no translation for the word hibernation.
Try... siesta grande!
¡CUATRO MESES!

DATELINE: PUERTO VALLARTA, MEXICO... THE YEAR OF THE SOUTHERN HIBERNATION BEGINS:
¿Desea tomar algo, señora?
zzzz
WOULD YOU LIKE SOMETHING TO DRINK, MADAM?

11-27-96
Un batido... con... miel de abejas para mí, por favor.
ONE MILKSHAKE WITH HONEY FOR ME, PLEASE.

Dos cervezas para estos osos.
Una margarita para este oso.
Si, señora.
zzzz
PINK FLOYD
TWO BEERS FOR THESE BEARS.
A MARGARITA FOR THIS BEAR.
YES, MADAM.
©Phil (CATCH THAT LIME DRIVE) Frank

MATT WILLIAMS! HOW COULD THE GIANTS TRADE MATT?
¡¡Señor!! Dos margaritas para este oso!
Si, señora.

THE TROPIC SUN FILTERS THROUGH THE PALMS THAT SURROUND THE HOTEL POOL ON THE SHORES OF PUERTO VALLARTA'S BAY. TWO BEARS SNOOZE AS HILDA READS A BODICE-RIPPER AND ALPHONSE...
YOU WANT TO KNOW THE WORST THING ABOUT THE GIANTS TRADING MATT WILLIAMS?
zzz zzzz

12-13-96
SEAGULLS WHIRL ABOVE AND GUITAR MUSIC DRIFTS ON THE WARM BREEZE:
Let's see now... What was the worst thing?
SLURRRRRP!
GIANTS

What were you saying, Alphonse?
Alphonse!
©Phil (TO SLEEP, PERCHANCE TO SNORE) Frank
Well... it's about time!
ZZZZZZZ